D1484888

PHILOSOPHICAL GEOMETRY

PHILOSOPHICAL GEOMETRY

ANDRÉ VANDENBROECK

INNER TRADITIONS INTERNATIONAL, LTD.
Rochester, Vermont

Inner Traditions International, Ltd.
Park Street
Rochester, Vermont 05767

Copyright ©1972, 1987 André VandenBroeck

First published by Sadhana Press, 1972

Distributed to the book trade in the United States by Harper & Row Publishers, Inc.

Distributed to the book trade in Canada by Book Center, Inc., Montreal, Quebec.

Library of Congress Cataloging-in-Publication Data

Vandenbroeck, André.
    Philosophical geometry.

    1. Geometry—Foundations.   I. Title.
QA681.V33 1987   516   86-20171
ISBN 0-89281-116-1 (pbk.)

Printed and bound in the United States of America

TABLE OF CONTENTS

to the masters

INTRODUCTORY NOTES CONCERNING PHILOSOPHICAL GEOMETRY

> Geometry is one and eternal, a reflection
> out of the mind of God. That mankind
> shares in it is one of the reasons to call
> man an image of God.
>
> *Johannes Kepler*
> (1571-1630)

I

Philosophical Geometry covers the activity of establishing a necessary conduct for mind through a set of signs denoting a necessary conduct of facts. To the extent that Philosophical Geometry describes phenomena, it proposes no Ideas which facts would represent; but to the extent that these facts are *necessary,* they imply law, and Philosophical Geometry transcends pure phenomenology. It is indeed in the *necessity* of the facts described that Philosophical Geometry seeks its value and aims at knowledge.

Thus Philosophical Geometry at once divides into facts and signs, into practice and theory, the former entirely contained within a two-dimensional universe, the latter within language. The particular universe assigned to Philosophical Geometry needs no defense, because necessity in facts can only be achieved within particular limits, and further, because Philosophical Geometry places its curiosity neither in knowledge nor in comprehension of a particular universe, but merely in the designata of necessary facts and in the comprehension and knowledge reached through the language which these facts promote. Philosophy is geometric only because nowhere have philosophers found necessity more compelling than in Geometry.

A priori defense of Philosophical Geometry as theory of language is more difficult; only the achieved discipline can justify this claim. But it will be immediately apparent that geometric facts present themselves ready-named, and if their name is called, will respond with proof of their identity, so that a set of signs can be evolved which accurately denotes a universe of facts. Such a set of signs would constitute perfect language, as signs conforming to a universe of facts offer the basis for a linguistic structure identical to a structure of experience. In a universe more general than the universe here proposed, language does not achieve this advantageous situation. In the gravitational universe, for instance, experience again and again conforms to the mathematical language expressing the laws of falling bodies, but in no way do bodies dictate a set of signs expressive of their fall. By induction, and in a language expressing concepts of time, space, mass, and motion (which a falling body might well *imply,* although never solicited for its experience), laws are worded to which any falling body must comply. These laws in turn convert into a syntax of signs chosen from a specialized language, or better, an existing language is syntactically fitted to the experience in order to spell out its law. At the root of this language but beyond our present concern, there festers a mere hypothesis as to the nature of the universe in which bodies fall. For the moment, we are merely bent on tracing signs, and we note that in the universe of physics, they stem from laws rather than from experience, while experience only *conforms* to signs. When physical experience is submitted to notation, it reduces to theoretical experiment.

Not so in Philosophical Geometry, where experience of fact and theory of language are carefully sundered from the start. Language here evolves from a set of signs dictated by an experience of absolute necessity, so that the order of signs can never be elsewhere applied. Necessity qualifies geometric facts, excluding all variants of experience, and no laws can be induced save a sole-singular law governing a unique experience, a law at best identical with the experience itself. It is then sufficient for Philosophical Geometry to note a set of signs promoted by the experience and to found a theory upon the language prefigured by these signs. The independence of these signs is noteworthy in opposition to other languages expressive of facts; not being a partial syntactic selection (as would be the law regulating the fall of bodies in the universe of physics), they convey no presuppositions and pertain fully and solely to the promotion of geometric facts. Where a falling body can never find independence from the total mass of the universe within which it is observed, Philosophical Geometry maintains the possibility of independent inception and necessary order: If there exists a syntax of signs that is expressive of a sequence of facts, and if it exists without former referents and without presuppositions, such a structural version of facts can be evolved by Philosophical Geometry.

Whatever the power of such a set of signs, it spends itself entirely on its structural endeavor and stays aloof from any problem of meaning. To extend such combinations beyond their mere horizontal order, a set of signs must clear the gap which separates it from a rightful place within language, a place, however, to which all sets of signs are not able to stake a claim. For language guarantees its foundation not only by the comprehension which its signs, as **terms**, afford, but by a formalization through grammar and syntax and through the inventory of a vocabulary. Unless a set of signs is covered by such referential instruments, it must remain in isolation, losing none of its horizontal structuring power, but destined to confine itself to an expression of order: extension beyond terminology is a prerogative of language and does not belong to an isolated set of signs. As a set of *terms,* language is a structural instrument, but when it anchors to its terms the far-floating meaning of **words**, it becomes an instrument of knowledge. A language of terms is built on comprehension and order, with general agreement a standing possibility depending only on agreement as to the referential instruments of grammar and syntax. Vocabularies, furthermore, unequivocally show a sign as being or not being a term. In language, the total set of terms as well as all possible orders are present at every moment.

But what of sets of signs which are not part of a formalized language? They are the matter of perception, and nature offers an infinite variety of such sets which remain the objects of pure intuition unless, at best, art imagines them into a natural language, or science harnesses them into natural law, while at worst, common sense dulls them into opaque stuff. In each of these transactions, an immeasurable hiatus gapes between the offer of the sign and the bid of human understanding, for in each case, signs are coerced by a syntactical order which no necessity commands: unless a set of signs promotes its language, no choice of language can be justified, as such justification in itself is part of language.

Briefly, then, sets of signs can be of three distinct types: those which represent names of facts given simultaneously with the facts, those which are parts of language, and those neither given with the facts nor referrable to language. The first in their entirety are covered by Philosophical Geometry, the second are the common food of human thought and reason, while the third are glyphs which vouchsafe our contact with reality.

II

WHY PHILOSOPHICAL GEOMETRY?

1. To contrast with axiomatic geometry.

    An axiomatic discipline is founded on a group of propositions considered self-evident or necessary, from which a chain of further propositions can be deduced. The validity of a set of axioms resides in the extent of the deductive chain permitted by the set. An axiom is superseded by another if the latter allows a more extensive chain of deductions.

    This method is open to criticism:

    a) The nature of self-evidence is debatable, and such debate ruins the very notion of self-evidence. The statement: "The whole is greater than any of its parts," a proposition frequently cited to instance the nature of axioms, can be taken as an example; such a statement is actually true only within a specific frame of reference, is not evident in itself, and becomes so only if further qualified.

    b) The necessity of the axioms proposed is determined before any knowledge of the discipline has been secured. Thus the mind imposes a necessity upon the object of investigation—a prejudice to all subsequent findings. It is obviously desirable to leave the discipline itself free to dictate its own necessities with minimum interference by the investigating mind. Propositions in geometry must be *geometrically* and not dialectically necessary. The aim of Philosophical Geometry is not toward a maximum number of deduced propositions, but toward minimal interference in a necessary state of affairs.

c) In axiomatic geometry, adequacy of axioms can be judged only after the chain of propositions is exhausted, a procedure akin to a trial and error method and dangerous to the faculties of mind which are constantly permitted to exert themselves on principles not yet proven to be adequate. Ideally, and from the very outset of investigation, the mind should be concerned with true propositions adequately related to the object of investigation.

2. Because geometry is the property of mind in general and not a specialty of the analytic mind and of its specific orientation.

a) In "Meno," Plato shows geometry as a birthright of mind in general: Meno's slave, unhampered by his lack of background, comprehends a geometric necessity with which Socrates confronts him. It will be remembered that the situation called for recognition of a square constructed upon the diagonal of another square as being twice the size of the latter.

b) Geometry is a study of necessary truths and concerns propositions necessarily true for mind in general. Although geometry, within restricted quarters, has grown into the backbone of analytic disciplines and away from its natural status as pure expression of mind in general, it is essential that an approach to pure geometry be furnished outside of the particular specialization of analytic disciplines.

3. Because Philosophical Geometry offers a guide to thought independent of personal opinion and of style, and because it proposes a language where every concept is shown in full extension, where every object can be correctly named, thus offering the possibility of adequate communication.

III

PHILOSOPHICAL GEOMETRY — SCIENCE, PHILOSOPHY, OR ART?

Nomenclature apparently assigns this discipline to philosophy and science. Geometry has historically been a field of interest to philosophers; since Descartes, it has been forged into a logical instrument to guide the various analytical specializations. Etymologically, geometry aims at a measure of the earth, but we cannot forget that to the Greek, Gaea is universe rather than planet, and that his gods tread the same earth as mortals do, though in greater elevation: an instrument to measure the earth could measure Mount Olympus. And it is manifest that Thales, Pythagoras, or Plato, all students of anthropocosmic thought such as it was presented in the temples of the Pharaohs, saw in this discipline more than a means for land surveying, more perhaps than a universal measure, but a measure of man's potentialities. They saw man as cosmic measure and geometry as the expression of man's faculty. Hence Plato, for his paradigm of inborn knowledge, chooses a geometric fact. It is revealing that within the realm of nature, or *physis,* the mind does not find the ready correspondence offered by geometry.

As link between cosmic necessity and the faculties of mind, geometry fades with the great medieval thinkers and dies abruptly with Descartes and analysis. This discipline now truly attaches itself to earth, serving in the investigation of matter. Philosophy, its guide lost to scientific method, is committed to speculations and opinions, and to systems coherent according to Aristotle's logical principles. Henceforth philosophic greatness is not measured by correspondence to truth or reality, but by ability to express Ideas. In the words of Jean Cocteau: "I consider that science is in a way a sequence of conflicting errors and that great philosophers live on only because they are writers of genius. It is evident that nothing Descartes says stands up, yet Descartes remains Descartes because he is a great writer."

Thus flowers an aesthetic age, an age of style where personal investigation leads the artist to a particular sense of beauty not necessarily coupled with a general truth. The visual arts come to the fore with intuitive representations of an object which science simultaneously tries to fathom by rational law. As opposite poles make manifest one single energy, so do art and science bear witness still to their common origin in the medieval philosopher who searched for confirmation of intuitive understanding through creative manipulation of matter in concordance with cosmic law, and termed his search an art, his God the great geometer. There remains, in the later split of philosophy, art, and science, a powerful interaction among the three domains. Logic, guiding-line of science, is largely a philosophic enterprise. The investigation of perspective in the Renaissance, the waning of realism and of portrait art with the advent of the camera, the study of vibrational phenomena and impressionistic styles, the impact of the technical age and its paraphernalia upon subjects and methods—these are the salient features of the interaction of science and art. At the turn of this century, as matter slips from the grasp of science, art loses its hold on subject, still retaining notions of form until the work of Heisenberg, de Broglie, and others dissolves all possibilities of a solid grip on matter. The search for non-Aristotelian logics, for non-Newtonian physics (the contradiction of the basic tenets of these disciplines), finds a most accurate resonance in the attempt of a nonrepresentational pictorial expression. As the limits of physics crumble along with the very notion of matter as such, the limits of art vanish in an accelerated rhythm of personal enterprise.

The fundamental difference between art and science at this juncture comes into play as every hypothesis to be incorporated into the scientific concept awaits an experimental confirmation, a safety valve unknown to art. It is symptomatic of our time's fevered imagination that the general public, intrigued by the scope of a scientific concept beyond its intellectual capacities, supports a vast succedaneum of pseudo-scientific ideas escaping the rigor of experimental proof: science fiction. As destitute of artistic intuition as it is of scientific intelligence, this same public demands a product which will not burden its comprehension with limits. It demands an *art fiction,* and in obedience to the fundamental economic law of supply and demand, an art fiction it receives. The artist, in his Promethean struggle with existing limitations, cannot exert his powers where limits cannot be defined, and he plays no role in the production and merchandising of art fiction.

It must be pointed out that art fiction, besides its status as an outstanding business venture, is not without value to the general public. Demanding no effort beyond an assertion of personality irrespective of any interest or merit of such personality, it is within easy reach of everyone; being impervious to any criticism as it does not obey to any standard, it relieves the manufacturer of all responsibility: in this connection, we note the prominent place held by refuse and decay in the manufacture of art fiction. Thus it constitutes a perfectly vacuous action useful in filling the blank created by increased leisure time. Under the largely theoretical guise of "self"-expression, art fiction is also of some avail to psychotherapy.

The creative urge to extend existing limits, which leads to the disintegration of the figurative arts, shows a facet of the personal search for knowledge in the absence of theological curbs and directives, a condition peculiar to Western man. Though senseless from highly evolved cultural points of view such as the ancient Chinese or the Pharaonic, for instance, where a rigid and impersonal canon offers a perennial framework within which the hand differs but never the spirit defining a discipline, the occidental experiment in art can yet be construed as an invaluable experience, provided its conclusion be correctly understood and artistic vitality be not squandered upon a concluded experiment, upon a corpse. Talent does not lament nor does it hover over decay: while in a field deserted by creative powers an indistinct and crowded caravan of minor personalities elbows its way to some transitory attention, Philosophical Geometry breaks to the fore and claims its eternal right to human genius.

THE TEXT

POSTULATE OF EXISTENCE

THERE EXISTS AN ENTITY DEFINABLE
BY GEOMETRIC REPRESENTATION.

Philosophical Geometry is introduced by the above postulate of existence.

The postulate presents entity; geometry defines it by re-presentation.

A postulate of existence proposes the existence of a definable entity.

As presented, the entity is undefined; definition through representation is a proposition necessary to geometry; it does not further qualify entity.

The definition is qualified as geometric; geometric definition can be said to be definitive.

A qualified representation of entity is best termed a *universe*.

The present postulate of existence proposes a geometric universe and knows no other universe.

CONSTRUCT Ia

POSTULATE OF EXISTENCE

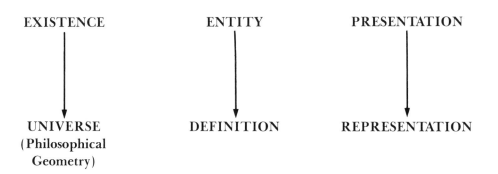

EXISTENCE   ENTITY   PRESENTATION

UNIVERSE   DEFINITION   REPRESENTATION
(Philosophical
Geometry)

CONSTRUCT Ib

THEORIA

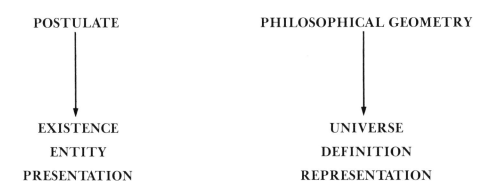

POSTULATE   PHILOSOPHICAL GEOMETRY

EXISTENCE   UNIVERSE
ENTITY   DEFINITION
PRESENTATION   REPRESENTATION

PHILOSOPHICAL GEOMETRY

THEORIA   A Postulate of Existence, as well as subsequent propositions of Philosophical Geometry, form a method best titled *theoria*.

PRACTICA   In Philosophical Geometry, geometric knowledge resides in a field of two-dimensional signs best termed *practica*.

PHILOSOPHICAL   Philosophy is an attribute of *theoria*, as geometry is of
GEOMETRY   *practica*.

CONSTRUCT Ic

PHILOSOPHICAL GEOMETRY

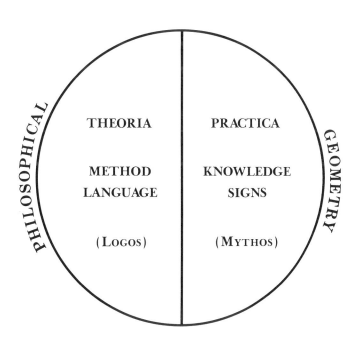

NOTE ON THEORIA

Theoria is the adequate expression of geometric experience. As such, it is dependent upon the perception of the geometer; it is a **subject**.

The aim of Philosophical Geometry is the individual elaboration of *theoria*, and the present *theoria* means to be no more than a map of terms and words toward the experience of Philosophical Geometry.

Practica is a necessary structure of two-dimensional events and is independent of the geometer's perception. It is the **object** of the discipline.

Theoria depends upon *practica* through the perception of the geometer, and it is due to the variance in *perception* that differences in *practica* occur.

PROPOSITIONS   *Theoria* consists of two types of propositions: Geometric propositions and logical propositions.

METHOD   Geometric propositions will be derived from elements of the geometric universe by means of an explicit method.

       Logical propositions will be derived from elements of a logical universe by means of an explicit method.

KNOWLEDGE-   Whereas non-geometric methods always *aim toward* or *lead*
STRUCTURE   *to* a knowledge-structure, geometric method has been shown to be a language *deriving from* a knowledge-structure.*

---

* *Connaissance et fonctions implicites* (Knowledge and Implicit Functions), unpublished paper, Bruges, 1959.

LOGICAL UNIVERSE

For *theoria* in Philosophical Geometry, a logical universe expresses itself by a set of *terms* each one of which has previously occurred in innumerable other sets. Such sets are perfectly comprehended by the syntactics: English vocabulary and grammar ("Syntactics: the science of combinations and order," cf. Cournot, *Traité de l'enchaînement des idées fondamentales dans les sciences et dans l'histoire*, Paris, 1861, as cited in Lalande's Philosophical Dictionary).

A postulate of existence concerning an entity definable by logical representation is not necessary to Philosophical Geometry as it is to metaphysics and other non-geometric philosophies. Philosophical Geometry admits language as preceding its discipline; it concedes pre-existence to language, thus giving it eternal presence.

Language as pre-existing is Logos. The pre-existing presence of language structures the logical universe into ordered sets of terms which are so many fragments of reality.

CONSTRUCT II

LOGICAL UNIVERSE

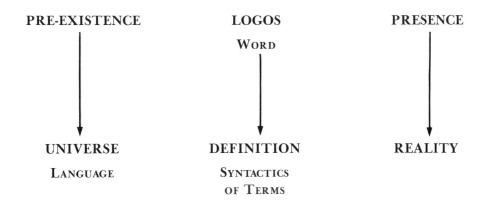

PRE-EXISTENCE	LOGOS WORD	PRESENCE
↓	↓	↓
UNIVERSE LANGUAGE	DEFINITION SYNTACTICS OF TERMS	REALITY

DEFINITIONS

DEFINITION

As Philosophical Geometry is definition in itself, no attempt is made within Philosophical Geometry to situate "definition" as a term.

Yet it must be remarked that in the geometric universe, definition (L. *finis*) is the limiting of the undefined, the negation of non-definition, whereas in the logical universe, definition lies in comprehension by means of **terms** (L. *terminus*). The operation in both cases reduces to **definition by contraction.**

GEOMETRIC
METHOD

In a geometric universe, names coincide and are simultaneous with events.

Whenever such names are situated into a logical universe, there exists a geometric proposition. Names are the intermediary between a geometric universe and a logical proposition.

In Philosophical Geometry, generic names will be drawn from letters of an alphabet, specific names from number. Any geometric element can be considered as unity and specifically as: 1.

NAMES
TERMS
WORDS
SYNTACTICS
STRUCTURE
COMMUNICATION

Whenever there is geometric definition, there exists a set of perfectly adequate terms expressive of that definition. Such terms are the **names** of geometric elements.

A **term** is the comprehension of a word, and a word can be perfectly comprehended in its term.

A **word** is the extension of a term, and the perfect extension of a term is not to be achieved.

Syntactics is the science of combinations and order. *Theoria* is structured upon the syntactics of English grammar and vocabulary.

Whenever a **structure** is based upon explicit syntactics, *communication* is perfectly possible.

Theoria is never concerned with words, and all logical propositions are syntactics of terms. We have seen that geometric propositions are syntactics involving geometric names.

Only terms and geometric names occur in *theoria*, and *theoria* is composed of two types of propositions only: logical and geometric propositions.

SITUATION

Postulation by *theoria* proposes entity as well as representation, but stipulates no relation between them.

Subsequent to presentation, any proposition re-presents.

Postulation by *theoria* cannot stipulate relation, as such stipulation constitutes a partial extension of definition.

Postulated entity lacks relation with any possible universe, and specifically with geometric representation.

Lack of relation cannot be encountered within a universe, or among objects, but can occur between universes, or among aggregates; it necessarily occurs between undefined entity and any universe of re-presentation.

By attribution, objects can always be related into aggregates, but the ensuing universe is strictly defined by the attribute of relation and such definition may or may not be partially or totally exclusive.

Total exclusivity between universes, or the particular exclusivity between entity and universe, form structures best termed *levels*.

Entity is not a universe, as it did not become through aggregation, but is presented by postulate.

Entity is independent; re-presentation is not only subsequent to presentation, it is dependent on entity. Dependence without relation is best termed *situation*.

Geometric definition is situated by a structure of levels identical to the structure of geometric propositions, so that all geometric propositions of *theoria* are situated within the field of *practica*.

Logical propositions of *theoria* are propositions necessary to Philosophical Geometry, but have no part in the structure of *practica*.

CHAOTIC UNIVERSE

Prior to Philosophical Geometry, the field of geometric definition is a two-dimensional universe containing all and every possibility of geometric representation prior to the notion of order (Figure 0).

GEOMETRIC ELEMENTS

Geometric elements represent geometric definition.

Practica allows existing geometric elements to appear in an inherent and necessary order.

FIRST GEOMETRIC ELEMENT

The first geometric element is doubly qualified: it is **first** and it is **geometric**.

Being first and geometric in *theoria*, it will be **simple** and **two-dimensional** in *practica*.*

DESIGNATION; SIGNIFICATION OF NAMES

Geometric elements are designated by letters of an alphabet, by number, and according to the principle of maximum economy. Simplicity and relative complexity of geometric elements appear in their designations. A simple element can be fully designated by one single letter of an alphabet.

INSCRIPTION

Practica results from inscriptions upon the two-dimensional field by means of an inscribing instrument best termed the *stylus*.

Inscriptions are adequately expressed by geometric propositions.

---

* The implication of **simplicity** in a **first** element requires a justification which is beyond the scope of this text. In *La Théorie Harmonique: le Principe de Simplicité dans les Mathématiques et dans les Sciences Physiques,* (Paris 1955), M. André Lamouche conclusively shows the intuitive need expressed by the notion of simplicity and, through historical collation as well as through the study of the notion itself, definitively justifies the postulate of a simple datum and a steady progression by degrees of maximum relative simplicity. It furthermore appears that on purely methodological grounds, Philosophical Geometry precludes an initial complexity.

PRACTICA

GEOMETRIC
GESTURE

On a homogeneous two-dimensional field best termed a *plane*, the stylus is posited in a gesture of inscription. The contact of stylus with plane breaks the homogeneity of the undifferentiated surface into a heterogeneity of the point of contact and the remainder of the plane.

Comment: The geometric gesture alone can initiate *practica*. Whatever the final complexity of inscription, the latter must pass through this initial stage: the contact of stylus with plane.

POINT

Contact of stylus with plane produces an inscription best termed a **point** (Figure 1).

Comment: There is no choice in terminology. Minimal contact of stylus and plane determines a marking which can only be described as "dot" or "point." In a geometric context, the latter term alone is adequate.

Hypothesis: The point is a first geometric element.

Verification and Discussion: If the point is a first geometric element, it must be 1) simple and 2) two-dimensional.

1) The point, ideally considered as an indivisible minimal marking showing position within the plane, can be fully designated by the single letter **a**. Thus considered, the point fulfills the condition of simplicity.

2) To qualify the point as a two-dimensional element is a contradiction in terms. A point cannot be a surface. If dimensionality is associated with the point, the latter must be considered as the limit of a volume indefinitely decreasing along each of its dimensions. As the point cannot be a surface, it fails to fulfill the condition of two-dimensionality.

Conclusion: The point is not a first geometric element.

MOTION

Practica can progress beyond the point only by motion of the stylus.

LINE

Motion of the stylus produces an inscription best termed a **line** (Figure 2).

Comment: Again the terminology is necessary. Whatever the direction or extent of the motion, the term "line" is most accurately attached to the resulting inscription.

Hypothesis: The line is a first geometric element.

Verification and Discussion: If the line is a first geometric element, it must be 1) simple and 2) two-dimensional.

1) The line considered as a distance between its two extremities can be fully designated by a single letter **a** expressing that distance. Thus considered, the line fulfills the condition of simplicity.

2) To qualify the line as a two-dimensional element is a contradiction in terms. A line cannot be a surface. And yet, contrary to the point, it cannot be considered an ideal indivisible marking. Although, as line, it cannot be a surface, it clings to the plane by a dimension of length and thus forces upon contemplation a second dimension of width which is the thickness of the inscribing stylus. Thus considered, the inscription appears as an elongated element whose length **a** differs from its width which must therefore be designated by a different letter, for example, **b**. As the element **ab**, the inscription becomes geometric. But by the same token, it loses its simplicity. Examination of the line thus shows that it is either simple but non-geometric or geometric but complex, and cannot be both simultaneously.

Conclusion: The line is not a first geometric element.

FACTORS
OF
CONTINGENCY

In order to maintain a necessary sequence of events in *practica*, all arbitrary circumstances or contingencies must be eliminated. In the foregoing examination of line, two contingencies are to be noted:

I — To examine the line, motion of stylus has to be arrested.

II — The width of the element **ab**, the dimension **b**, is contingent upon the width of the stylus.

Ia — If the motion of stylus is not arrested, a continuous line results. This uniform, indefinitely prolonged motion of stylus finds its perfect representation only in the circle.

Continuous uniform motion of stylus produces an inscription best termed a **circle** (Figure 3).

IIa — In order to eliminate the arbitrary dimension of the line, the length of the line can be considered equal to the width of the stylus.

Motion of stylus limited to the width of the stylus can be termed *minimal motion.*

Minimal motion of stylus produces an inscription best termed a *square* (Figure 4).

The side of a square is best termed the *root.*

Ib — **Hypothesis:** The circle is a first geometric element.

Verification and Discussion: If the circle is a first geometric element, it must be 1) simple and 2) two-dimensional.

1) The circle can be designated by its center, an ideal point equidistant from all points on the circle. The center directs the circle. It can be designated by one single letter **a**.

2) The circle can be considered as the limit of a circular surface.

IIb — **Hypothesis:** The square is a first geometric element.

Verification and Discussion: If the square is a first geometric element, it must be 1) simple and 2) two-dimensional.

1) — 2): The square can be designated by the length of its root **a**. The square of root **a** is termed: a^2. The numeral 2 does not imply complexity, it merely indicates the two-dimensional nature of **a**. The designation a^2 expresses the simplicity as well as the two-dimensionality of the square.

Conclusion: Both circle and square appear as geometric elements as soon as motion produces line. No precedence can be given to one over the other.

GEOMETRY
AND
HARMONY

As a first element of a discipline must be a single element, Philosophical Geometry at this moment divides into two fields of study: *geometry*, whose first element is the square, and *harmony* whose first element is the circle. These two disciplines are to be developed in close correlation.

SCALAR
UNIVERSE
OF
GEOMETRY

The square as shown in Figure 4 is a theoretical representation. Practically, the root of the square must be represented as surface in order to gain existence on the plane (Figure 5), and each ensuing root must obey the same necessity (Figure 6). Thus the plane develops into a **geometric grid** (Figure 7), contributing to the two-dimensional universe the attribute of **scale**. In retrospect, it can be seen that from the posited point, through motion and its arrest, to the square and its further development, a continuity finds its first resting place only with the concept of the scalar universe of geometry, i.e., in pure multiplicity or number.

Since any geometric representation must first cover the development from point to scalar universe, all subsequent geometric representations will be initiated at the scalar level.

THOUGHTS ON SCALE

For Philosophical Geometry, and from within a two-dimensional practice, a scalar formation first signifies **reason**—the possible *knowledge* of a geometric universe the existence of which is proposed by postulate. It throws a light upon an entity definable by such representation and it compels the mind in the true meaning of *necessity*: the scalar universe is immediately and absolutely free of magnitude, the understanding adhering to a qualitative structure in leisurely contemplation of an idea. The geometric grid furnishes in fact the entire metaphysics which its becoming has implied; situated as close to absolute beginning as the mind can symbolize, it must yield the essence of the discipline. Here art joins calculation as creative substance, and these crossroads of freedom and necessity mark the moment before **measure**, the most aesthetic instance of Philosophical Geometry.

In the establishment of scale, all quantitative concerns are left in three-dimensional hands, well outside the specific limits of Philosophical Geometry. They touch upon space, convenience, and whatever other arbitrary components, totally alien to our discipline, may enter into a technique which gives it presence.*

Scale is specifically adaptable to subsequent figurations and is best chosen *after* the event. By the same token, a preferential range of scale exists for any event, but never does the necessity of the event depend upon its scale.† Through scale, quantity is absorbed into a more profound understanding of a sameness neither identical nor equal: **similarity** is a difference of scale only, and where number is concerned, regular polygons present a natural opportunity for such qualitative conduct.

---

* The manipulations in themselves, physical or mental, are of interest solely because they show a *labor* in overlapping raw experience and evolved reality, a technique of mind as well as of hand.

† A constant, though mainly silent pervasiveness of scale, making itself heard only in actual measure, most clearly shows in the intuitive use of quadriled paper for clarity in the simplest expression of plane geometry.

NOTE ON HARMONY*

Whereas geometric definition is confined to a field of two dimensions, harmony is an intrinsic part of the three dimensional vibratory universe.

For Philosophical Geometry, the source of the harmonic phenomenon is the vibrating string which can be perfectly represented and studied in the present discipline. The study of the auditive function as receptor of the harmonic phenomenon is not part of Philosophical Geometry, although the human ear plays an instrumental role in the cognizance of the events. Concerning the organ of harmony, one salient capacity lacking in the other four sensory organs must be brought out: its perfect judgment of harmonic interval. No other organ can reduce a chaotic universe of time, space, quality, or quantity into a **natural scalar universe**, and the auditive function alone furnishes names and measure along with vibratory data. Sound is volume, a "spherical propagation in all directions through the atmosphere which fills all surrounding space" (Helmholz). Thus the scalar universe of harmony is three-dimensional, conceivable as a vertical dimension of harmonics or overtones†—a horizontal dimension of interval and the third dimension of sound reaching the ear.

In harmony, plucking the string corresponds to positing the point in geometry. All subsequent data derives from that harmonic gesture and its perception by the ear; the scalar universe of harmony.

SITUATION OF HARMONY
The circle (Figure 3) combines Figures 1 and 2 into an initial harmonic representation. All subsequent representations in the field of harmony will concern Figure 3 or sections of Figure 3. Figure 3, and thus the entire field of harmonic definition, is situated by a structure of levels identical to the structure of logical propositions, so that all harmonic propositions of *theoria* are situated within fact as well as reality.

---

* The technical aspects of sound, harmony, and audition are thoroughly covered by Helmholtz in his classic work "On the Sensations of Tone." The only facts recalled here will be those essential to the understanding of the notion of harmony within the context of Philosophical Geometry.

† The plucked string produces a fundamental tone and a series of secondary, higher-pitched overtones or harmonics. The study of these harmonics and their relationships precisely delineates the field of harmony in Philosophical Geometry.

LINE AS VIBRATING STRING	The line which was rejected as geometric element is seen to be a perfect representation of the vibrating string. It always represents a section of a circle.*
POINT AS RULE	Also rejected as geometric element, the point, a constant equidistance from the circle, achieves existence through its functional rule over harmonic representation.

---

* It is remarkable that reality, as a word, can take a fuller extension when the term is attributed to harmony rather than to geometry as such. It is by the vibrating string and its **volume** that Philosophical Geometry achieves its grasp on reality. The string, however, can be measured only by geometry.

SQUARE AND DIAGONAL

POTENTIAL
OF
GEOMETRIC
ELEMENT

The square contains a potential element: its diagonal.

I. It is evident that the square contains twice this potential element and, in a square, diagonals are equal, their study leading to identical conclusions. It is therefore sufficient to examine one single diagonal in all its consequences, save in the present intersection where it plays its part in an intuitive center of a circle potentially quartered by the square. Here the full potential of a first geometric element is actually expressed (Figure 8).*

UNITY OF
ELEMENT

II. Any geometric element can act as unity. In numbers, its essential aspect is then equal to 1.†

RELATION
OF
ROOT
TO
SQUARE

III. Given with square and diagonal is the evidence that root and diagonal are functionally related. By the same path which brought into existence a first square, the full potential of the diagonal is to be expressed by showing it in its turn as the root of a square (Figure 9).‡

---

* As can be shown in the completed discipline, this actuality in turn contains the full potential of Philosophical Geometry. From stage to stage and from level to level, no element has entered the field after the original contact and its motion. There has been only actualizing of potential in creative action, the purest conduct of the intellect and motive of Philosophical Geometry.

† An immediate instance is proposed by the geometric grid, any unit square of which can have its root equal 1.

‡ The process brings into existence a second grid inclined by the constancy of the diagonal. The relation of both grids is evident: it is the relation of similarity, a sameness neither identical nor equal.

When relating root and diagonal of square 1, identical elements are related, namely root : root. As the square built on the diagonal must in turn have a diagonal, we form the same logically compelling relation in terms of diagonal : diagonal. Homogeneity of concept cannot be put in doubt with such identical relations of terms, and it binds not only root to root and diagonal to diagonal, but root to diagonal as well (and diagonal to root), into a structure of similarity the terms of which are grouped into relations of relations.

$$\frac{root}{root} : \frac{diagonal}{diagonal}$$

$$\frac{root}{diagonal} : \frac{root}{diagonal}$$

PROLIFERATION OF NUMBER

IV. The relation of square 1 to a square the root of which is diagonal to square 1 is intuitively evident as 1 : 2 (Figure 10). By recognizing in each subsequent square a diagonal which in turn gives rise to a square, a series of relations appears on the grid (Figure 11).

$$\frac{root\ of\ square\ 1}{root\ of\ square\ 2} : \frac{root\ of\ square\ 2}{root\ of\ square\ 4}$$

where the **extreme terms** "root of square 1" and "root of square 4" are clearly legible as:

root of square 1 = 1

root of square 4 = 2

whereas **the mean term** "root of square 2" cannot be further enlightened by the grid. It remains the identity of "diagonal of square 1" to "root of square 2." No number is here forthcoming by the agency of measure, nor any manipulation which could make the "diagonal of square 1" more comprehensible than as "root of square 2." A **function** is expressed creative of **number** without itself being tied to the specificity of it. This function is indicated by the replacement symbol: $\sqrt{}$, standing for "root of square," and used to denote squares of which the root is comprehensible only as diagonal. The series of relations above shows the first step of a proliferation of numbers by squares and the function which is the agent of proliferation, the former comprehended by grouping relations as squares:

$$\frac{1}{2} \; : \; \frac{2}{4},$$

the second by showing the diagonal as mean:

$$\frac{1}{\sqrt{2}} \; : \; \frac{\sqrt{2}}{2}.$$

Proliferation is expressed in general terms by the proportionate measure:

$$\frac{c}{b} \; : \; \frac{b}{a}.$$

ON PROPORTION

THE LOGICAL EXISTENCE OF PHILOSOPHIC MEASURE IN GEOMETRY

The action of the diagonal within square 1 or 1^2 performs a geometric scission of unity through which the scalar universe, the chaos of number, is ordered into a universe of **measure**. A number of elements appear, there exists relation among them, and comparison of these relations leads to measure. In general terms, if there exists a number of elements: **a, b, c, d, e, f,** . . . and a relation can be found among them so that **b** stands in relation to **a**, or $\frac{b}{a}$ or **b: a**, and **d** stands in relation to **c** or $\frac{d}{c}$ or **d : c**, then a relation might exist between these relations so that **b** has the relation to **a** which **d** has to **c**, in other words: **b** is to **a** as **d** is to **c** or $\frac{b}{a} : \frac{d}{c}$ or **b : a :: d : c**.

Such an expression is a proportionate measure and Philosophical Geometry knows no other; a relation of relations is best termed **proportion** whenever the intent is measure.

The scission of unity initiates measurable multiplicity; the full expansion of the first geometric element shows the diagonal to the square identical to the diameter of the circle not only as geometric fact, but functionally as well, for it is intuitively certain that as the square is halved by a diagonal, so is the circle by a diameter (Figure 12). Yet, even when fully expressed (Figure 13), circle and diameter yield no more than the original datum: an internal division and a relation 1 : 1.*

Although there is division in two parts, there is no generation of number, and the idea of true scissiparity is at this level reserved for the square-diagonal and its geometric proliferation:

$$1, 2, 4, 8, 16, 32, 64, \ldots .$$

---

* There is a fruitful lesson in the contrast between square-diagonal and circle-diameter when expanded onto the grid; the former opens on an avenue to geometric conduct, the latter only repeats itself into a decorative motif which in no way furthers the geometric discipline, unless it be by reiterating the basic scalar grid.

Circle-diameter acts as mean term between unity and duality* in a distinctive representation of **duality within unity**. The event and its propensity toward proliferation are contained by the unitary circle, and no multiplicity ensues, as it does when a diagonal $\sqrt{2}$ projects duality beyond itself (Figure 14); for the latter event there exists a logically perfect graph which clearly shows the separate levels, exterior one to another, of unity, duality, and subsequent generations in the ratio of their proliferation (Table I).† Both circle-diameter and square-diagonal, by representing the effects respectively of a first division and a first multiplication, signify the existence of 1 and of 2, and of the relation ½ or 1 : 2. The latter are dual expressions for an identical function, but are manifested on the one hand as a fractioned whole and on the other as a confrontation of integers transmitting objectivity and magnitude. Such differentiations in language are to be explored whenever they correspond to a definition of well-founded events in *practica*, as in the case which occupies us here. Although the expressions are identical in their consequence for calculation, they are not so in their conduct of mind, as unity remains a comprehending circumference for the circle, whereas it degenerates, by proliferation, into a mere unit of magnitude multiplying itself into numbers.‡

Geometric progression by dichotomy, such as it can be graphically shown in Table I, achieves clear limitation between unity and duality by the agency of trinity, or 3. The numbering unit, counting the three parts, does not claim jurisdiction over their relation one to another as magnitudes. It merely certifies the image of 3 as two units viewed together with 1 as one unit, concerned only with their clear separation, not with their origin one from another. On the other hand, the image of trinity is not formed when duality is viewed within unity. The image of the diametered circle cannot coerce the mind toward trinity, as it never detaches duality from unity into a tripartite statement: it retains the relation expressed by ½, therefore declaring two equal parts of 1. Not so dichotomy, where the asymmetry of three given parts permits an unequal scission into 1/3 and 2/3, an expression of scale, as

$$\frac{1}{3} \; : \; \frac{2}{3} \; : \quad : \; 1 \; : \; 2$$

shows the relation of 1 to 2 in a trinitary context, or with a common denominator of 3.

---

* In keeping with its harmonic destiny, the entire field of harmony will be seen to reside between 1 and 2.

† Unity dichotomizing *outside* of itself, and duality *situated* in relation to unity.

‡ The insistence in Pharaonic Egypt on a functional system valorizing a unitary numerator reflects a necessity for the government of unity over any multiplicity, a necessity rigid enough to be called theological.

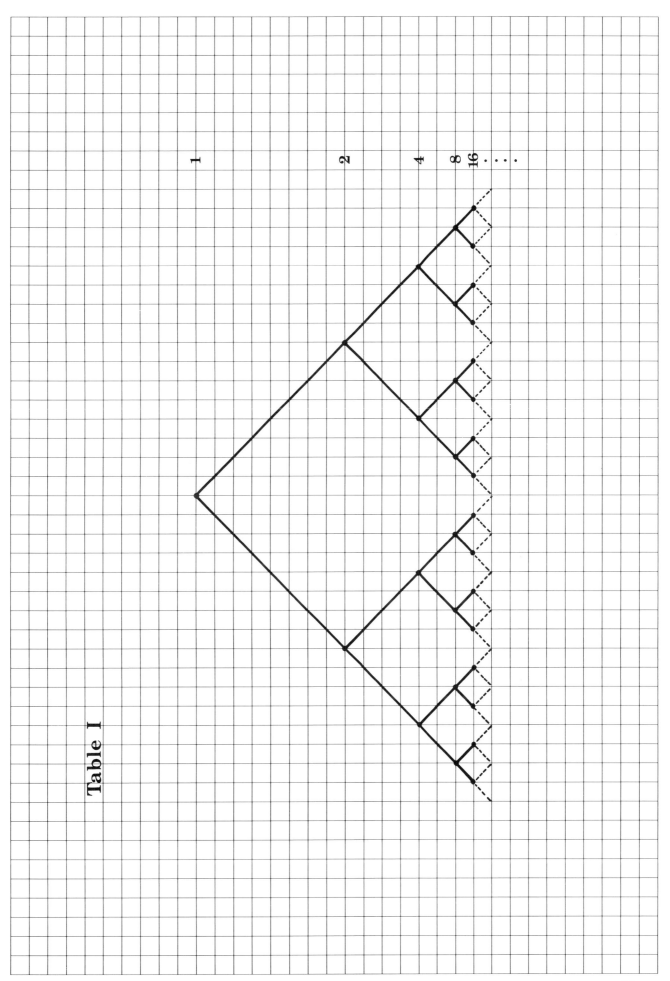

Table I

1
2
4
8
16 . . . . .

The division of unity into equal parts by the diametered circle is a first phenomenon of harmony. If a relation is sought between the equal parts, it will be a unitary relation, as **a** : **a**, or 1 : 1.* The attribute of duality within unity is best termed *identity;* the relation of unitary parts: *equality.*† However complex their generic nomenclature, equal parts, when related, accept unity as their simplest specification. The relation remains within unity, cannot proliferate, produces no number; duality can be seen as the extreme development—the end of this scission within unity—so that the entire harmonic universe is situated between 1 and 2.

The necessity rooted in the square-diagonal to project duality out of unity as a first phenomenon of geometry induces the logical conduct of the dichotomous diagram in Table I. Thereby an **order** of logical operations is established with the dual primacy of division-multiplication tied to circle and square in *practica* where the necessity of an immediate scission in a first element already stands corroborated.

---

* "Creation, the Present Moment, is without limit, but concretization knows a finality, a limit which is the Ego, **a** : **a** as function, the thing facing itself." R.A. Schwaller de Lubicz, "Verbe Nature" in *Aor*, Paris 1963, p. 191.

† *Footnote on Notation:* Identity is indicated by the sign ≡, for example, A ≡ A, and since identical elements can always be related, their equality can be shown by the sign = , for example, A = B. A further degradation of unity obtains with relations in function of 1. These expressions are usually written as equalities, but are geometrically of a quite different nature and must be distinguished. Thus, for example, the binomial equation

$$(a + b)^2 = a^2 + 2ab + b^2$$

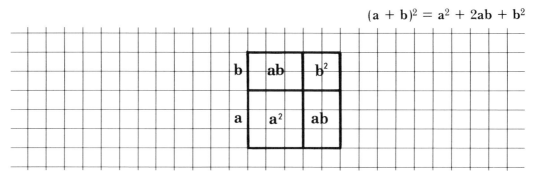

shows on one side the roots of a square. On the other side, four areas (two of which are *equal*, thus furnishing a definition of geometric equality), show a heterogeneity which is better comprehended as a relation in function of unity and expressed

$$\frac{(a + b)^2}{a^2 + 2ab + b^2} = 1 \, .$$

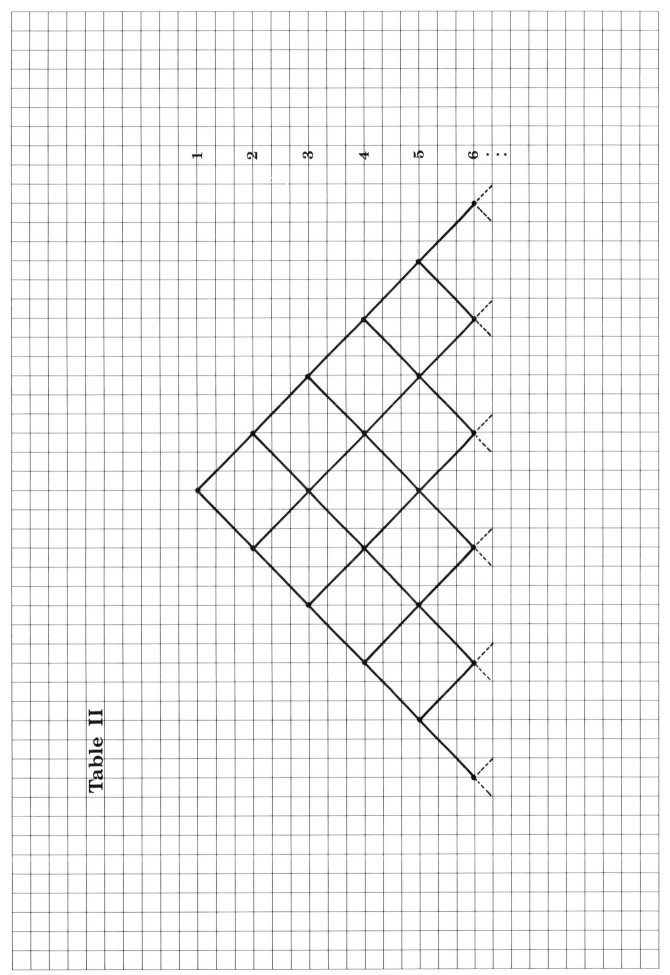

Table II

1
2
3
4
5
6 · · ·

It cannot be objected that the numerating principle of dichotomy is no more than *selectively* creative of number, for as soon as the mind chooses to control the dichotomous proliferation (*choosing*, it leaves the apodictic path of pure geometry to enter a logic where choice is endemic), it realizes the conjunctive possibilities of the dichotomized, as when unity divides in the multiplication by 2, creating, for instance, A < B, and visualizes A + B = 1. Addition, a tertiary operation after division and multiplication, is immediately coupled to negation as its prime consequence. There are now *two* units which can be together as A + B. One can also be *without* the other in the disjunction of A or B, meaning either A or B, but not both (the latter case being covered by the addition A + B). As addition moves conjunction because it is the principle which reunites, so negation is the ground of disjunction, for if there is choice in duality, the one is chosen at the loss of the ineffective other.

The corrective imposed by reason upon dichotomous proliferation modifies Table I into Table II. There exists, within a constant division of unity into A and B resulting in a constant possibility of A + B = 1, the controlled complexity of a **lattice** where every point of intersection is a choice of A or B, meaning either A or B, but not both. Here again are shown the separate levels, exterior one to another, of unity, duality, and subsequent generations. Although effected by division, the principle of their controlled proliferation is most readily comprehended in the ordered series of natural number: 1, 2, 3, 4, 5, 6, 7, . . .

In the geometric concept of proliferating dichotomy, there must be a scission of unity into two unequal parts, as the dichotomy does not remain within unity. If the dichotomized parts cannot be related as 1 : 1, what relation, then, exists between those unequal parts? And to what extent does the proposition **c** < **b** imply a quantitative relation? These questions, among others, are answered by the involvement of **c/b** in a geometric measure, or proportion, for two given terms have but one representative measure where the small term is to the large term as the large term is to the sum of both, or

$$\frac{c}{b} \; : \; \frac{b}{c + b}.$$

Where only two terms exist, they must result from the dichotomy and their addition is equal to the initial one, or c + b = 1, so that

$$\frac{c}{b} \; : \; \frac{b}{1}.$$

This proportion is usually referred to as the "Golden Mean" and named by the Greek letter ϕ (Phi).

ϕ remains contained in a oneness restored by the conjunction of its two unequal terms: although it arises from duality and at the second level of dichotomy, its operation needs unity as an extreme term, and it achieves this oneness by reforming a unity of small part and large. Therefore it is the functional mean term between rational oneness* and the multiplicity of number. It participates in both, and though it has left oneness for the duality of unequal parts, it does not give rise to number beyond this initial scission. With duality in unity it shares a homogeneity owed to the unitary reference, here prescribed by the economy of terms and achieved by conjunction, there precluded by the symmetry of terms which eliminates all possibility of heterogeneity from the start. All and any duality within unity is identical, a first and most universal manifestation of One. ϕ, the proportion closest to unity, although its homogeneity is to an extent degraded by its asymmetric terms, still retains an unqualified sameness which makes all and any ϕ proportion similar to all others. They differ in scale only (a differentiation not attained by duality in unity, hence its lack of measure), and are tied to the identity of the relation of small part to large. There can exist only *one* measure of two unequal parts, but this measure is applicable to dichotomies on all levels of existence. In Philosophical Geometry, the first expression of this function of scissiparity is the diagonal to the square.

With multiplicity , ϕ holds in common the form of its proportional expression, or simpler yet and more immediately, its very expressiveness as measure. ϕ opens the possibility of measure, and thereby allies itself with all subsequent measure, particularly with the geometric proportion

$$\frac{c}{b} \ : \ \frac{b}{a}$$

of which it is but one specific case, the case where a = b + c. The course of generalization finds its logical end (as well as a possibility of measure within optimum disparity of elements) in the final heterogeneity of the four-term proportion

$$\frac{b}{a} \ : \ \frac{d}{c}$$

of which the geometric proportion is but a specific case, the case where a = d.† This progressive liberalization of the link by which four terms can serve the knowledge of each one through their position to each other, structures a pyramidal degradation of necessity from apical unity to the width of field staked out by the permissiveness of four disparate terms. This most general measure must lay bare the necessary minimum still giving significance to the proportional group, the quality below which there would exist no measure.

---

* Absolute unity is irrational, as an exterior reason would signify duality *ipso facto.*

† Harmonic proportions are an *application* of four-term proportions; they do not open further levels of generality.

To recapitulate, we can now retrace our steps starting from the base of maximum choice, the four-term proportion, to the unitary summit of necessity. In the geometric proportion, an inner cohesion was immediately established by the identical mean term also evident in ϕ, a feature to which the latter adds its reference to unity for a further tightening of context. Above ϕ, stringency allows no measure to emerge from oneness, though unity be rationalized by duality before it is finally absorbed into the irrational apex, the true point.

What then, is this quality present in all measure as its backbone, but most clearly felt in four-term proportions where it sustains alone the reason of the group? Best termed *ratio*, itself a relation of two terms which may or may not play a role in the proportion, it shows the model under which the measure is celebrated by ratio itself and by its multiples, or by its multiples alone, with ratio as generic comprehension.

To be distinguished in the pyramidal structure of proportion are the following levels:

    I — Unity, the point of the irrational.

    II — A metaphysical level of unity conceived through duality.

    III — An archetypical level showing the principle of measure by agency of ϕ.

    IV — A typical level in its two aspects of becoming and of being:

        a) the continuous geometric proportion as dynamic progression and

        b) the static four-term proportion as function of ratio.

DIMENSIONS OF HARMONY

MONOCHORD

The vertical dimension of harmony comes into existence with the plucking of the string and essentially furnishes all the elements of harmony. The eye discerns the harmonic motion of the string, while the ear detects a series of partials* within the whole sound. The string vibrates not only in its entirety, but simultaneously in a series of segments of decreasing length. It vibrates first and essentially as a whole, secondly as two halves, thirdly as three thirds, fourthly as four fourths and so on.† These various vibrating segments can be translated into the horizontal dimension of harmony by means of the monochord, a string stretched over a sounding board equipped with a scale and a movable stop, so that the string can be stopped at various fractions of its length, creating various intervals expressive of various **distances**.

---

* **Note on Harmonic Nomenclature:** The fundamental tone and the harmonics or overtones are all parts of the tone heard when the string is plucked. Thus they are correctly termed partials. (See Helmholtz, p. 22).

† The fundamental tone created by the vibrating of the entire string is the first partial, the overtone created by the vibrating of the half string is the second partial, so that:

Name	String-Length	Vibration
1st partial	1	1
2nd partial	1/2	2
3rd partial	1/3	3
4th partial	1/4	4
— — — —	— —	—
— — — —	— —	—

The sixteen first partials are necessary and sufficient to establish the laws of harmony.

NOTE ON DISTANCE

Whenever unity dichotomizes, it creates distance by creating 2. The fact that measurable intervals exist between 1 and 2 is sufficient evidence to postulate such a distance. No distance is ever covered in one step, for if it were, all possibility of measure would disappear. Now the distance between 1 and 2 is measurable, such measure being precisely the context of the study of harmony in Philosophical Geometry. Whenever there is distance, then, there is the necessity for a mean term, or a set of mean terms upon which the measure leans while bridging the gap. The purpose of the mean term or terms is to form a chain of relations in order to relate two extreme terms which, related to each other immediately, do not yield a measure.* Thus the mean term must be related to each of the extremes, or, in the case of a set of mean terms, the extremes must be related to each other by a design of interrelations† of means and extremes.

---

* Indeed, only a ϕ proportion could be set up between the extreme terms of the distance, which would show a function, but would contribute no number toward measure.

† It follows that a proportionate measure is a measure using a mean term or a set of mean terms, and that all proportionate measures indicate an instance of unity dichotomizing.

PROGRESSIONS*

The plucking of the string leads directly to two series of numbers, one the inverse of the other:

Vibrations: 1, 2, 3, 4, 5, 6, . . .

String-length: $1, \dfrac{1}{2}, \dfrac{1}{3}, \dfrac{1}{4}, \dfrac{1}{5}, \dfrac{1}{6}, \ldots$

ARITHMETIC

Vibrations yield an **arithmetic progression**†, with equality of difference between successive terms‡ as essential character:

progress arithmetically, then

$$\text{if} \quad b < q < a$$

$$q - b = a - q.$$

It follows that

$$2q = a + b$$

and

$$q = \frac{a + b}{2}$$

showing the mean term equal to half the sum of the extremes, the measure of **average**:

$$\frac{a + b}{2} : \frac{q}{1}.$$

In arithmetic measure, the relation to duality of the sum of the extremes is as the relation of the mean to unity. From this we draw:

$$\frac{q}{a + b} : \frac{1}{2}$$

in a reference to relation within unity.

---

* For the mathematics of proportions, cf. Paul-Henri Michel, *De Pythagore à Euclide: Contribution à l'Histoire des Mathèmatiques Préeuclidiennes,* Paris, 1950.

† cf. Table II: arithmetic progression by dichotomy.

‡ In a three-term progression or proportion, the mean term is usually designated as **q**, the large and small extremes as **a** and **b** respectively. Particular cases may form exceptions in nomenclature, such as the case of equality of square and rectangle $b^2 = ac$, where the mean term **b** is root of square.

The arithmetic measure permits a proportion with the relation 1 : 2, offering its three terms the possibility of grouping themselves as a relation within unity.

Harmony bypasses geometric proliferation in the creation of number and retains contact with unity by **averaging**.

HARMONIC

String length yields an harmonic progression characterized by an equality of relations or ratios:

$$\text{If} \quad b < q < a$$

progress harmonically, then the difference between the first two terms stands in the same relation to the first term as the difference between the second and third terms stands to the third:

$$\frac{q - b}{b} : \frac{a - q}{a} = \frac{n}{m}$$

which implies

$$\frac{q - b}{a - q} : \frac{b}{a}$$

and also

$$a(q - b) = b(a - q) \rightarrow aq - ab = ab - bq$$
$$\rightarrow \quad q(a + b) = 2ab.$$

The mean term in an harmonic proportion is thus expressible in terms of the extremes as

$$q = \frac{2\,ab}{a + b}.$$

The nature of the relation $\frac{n}{m}$ can be explicated by a closer examination of the harmonic characteristic

$$\frac{q - b}{b} : \frac{a - q}{a} = \frac{n}{m}.$$

38

According to the proportion:

$$\frac{n}{m} = \frac{q - b}{b}$$

and

$$\frac{n}{m} = \frac{a - q}{a}.$$

Solving for **q** in both cases, first in terms of **b** :

$$\frac{q - b}{b} = \frac{n}{m}$$

$$q - b = \frac{bn}{m}$$

$$\boxed{q = b + \frac{n}{m}\, b}$$

then in terms of **a** :

$$\frac{a - q}{a} = \frac{n}{m}$$

$$a - q = \frac{an}{m}$$

$$a - \frac{n}{m}\, a = q$$

$$\boxed{q = a - \frac{n}{m}\, a.}$$

We see that the mean term **q** can be expressed as the small term **b** plus a fraction of **b** as well as the large term **a** minus the identical fraction of **a**. $\frac{n}{m}$ is the fraction of themselves which **b** adds and **a** subtracts in order to compute the mean term q.

It follows that

$$b + \frac{n}{m} b = a - \frac{n}{m} a$$

$$b \left(1 + \frac{n}{m} \right) = a \left(1 - \frac{n}{m} \right)$$

$$\frac{b}{a} = \frac{1 - \dfrac{n}{m}}{1 + \dfrac{n}{m}} \rightarrow \frac{\dfrac{m - n}{m}}{\dfrac{m + n}{m}}$$

$$\boxed{\frac{b}{a} = \frac{m - n}{m + n}}$$

$$b + \frac{n}{m} b = a - \frac{n}{m} a$$

$$\frac{n}{m} b + \frac{n}{m} a = a - b$$

$$\frac{n}{m} (b + a) = a - b$$

$$\boxed{\frac{n}{m} = \frac{a - b}{a + b}.}$$

40

ANGLES

RIGHT
ANGLE*

The geometric grid (the scalar universe of Philosophical Geometry) can be viewed purely as a specific structure of right angles, herewith defining right angles in general. The square then becomes the quadrangular unit, and it is evident† that the diagonal to the square divides the latter into two identical‡ right triangles, being triangles containing one right angle. The two acute angles in each triangle must add up to a right angle to fulfill the condition of halving the square.

ACUTE
ANGLE

The scission of unity by the action of the diagonal within the square creates a right triangle with horizontal base 1, vertical cathetus 1, and diagonal hypotenuse $\sqrt{2}$ (Figure 15).**

MEASURE
OF
ANGLE

The right triangle permits the measure of all angles by relating cathetus to base.

The diagonal of the square thus constitutes angular unity:

$$\frac{\text{cathetus}}{\text{base}} = \frac{\overset{\wedge}{1}}{1} = \overset{\wedge}{1}$$

All angles are measured as fractions of 1 and exist within a triangular system.

---

* R.A. Schwaller de Lubicz, *Le Temple de l'Homme*, Editions Caractères, Paris 1957. Volume I, pgs. 297ff. *La Trigonometrie Pharaonique.*

† The notion of evidence enters Philosophical Geometry as a consequence of the square and its diagonal. It is the closest attribute of *practica* and basic to any pedagogic aims of the discipline. Concerned with reality rather than truth, it must be apparent to intuition and cannot be gleaned from propositions. Evidence in Philosophical Geometry lies purely in geometric elements and their becoming.

‡ The concern here is not the proliferating function of the diagonal but the conceptual grasp of "sameness" expressed by duality within unity.

** Rigorous conduct would express all surfaces, forming a grid of two systems related as $1 : \sqrt{2}$. Such developed figurations are implied whenever clarity demands reduced expressions to underline the essential elements under discussion.

In the right triangle, the sides which form the right angle (called "base" and "cathetus" when they relate in the nomenclature of angles) are equal only when naming $\overset{\wedge}{1}$. Choice in this case is indifferent between them with respect to service as cathetus or base.

Equally indifferent is the choice of referent for the measure. Both angles (which along with the right angle constitute the triangular system) are unitary, facing the sustaining right angle from identical points of view. They show duality within unity in a system of three angles. The function of the third element (the right angle) can be considered a mere mechanical measuring device, or else a more inclusive unity without measure, summing up a lower unitary level where duality has become possible.

ANGLE
AND
COMPLEMENT

Thus an angle never exists in isolation, but within the system of the three angles of a right triangle whose right angle stands for the possibility of measure, and the third angle as **complement** to the measured angle. Within the measure, this complement expresses itself as an inverse relation, for if the measure of an angle is expressed as

$$\frac{\text{cathetus}}{\text{base}} = \frac{b}{a}$$

then its complementary angle within the right triangle will be expressed as

$$\frac{\text{cathetus}}{\text{base}} = \frac{a}{b}.$$

In the measure of $\overset{\wedge}{1}$ where $\mathbf{a} = \mathbf{b}$, there is identity between complement and angle,* so that the duality retracts into unity. But in all other angular measures, the angle is inversed into its complement. And because the angle by definition is a fraction of unity, the complement is always $> \overset{\wedge}{1}$ and thus creative of pure multiplicity.

---

* By "angle" is henceforth meant the *measured* angle. There is indeed no need to particularize the "measured" angle, as there will always be only one measurable angle in any given triangle, one complement falling outside the definition of angles by being $> \overset{\wedge}{1}$ and a right angle with purely functional character.

42

True geometric measure is an expression of proportionality and angular measure is achieved by a second angular relation $\frac{\hat{b}'}{a'}$ which, related to $\frac{\hat{b}}{a}$, forms the desired proportion:

$$\frac{\hat{b}}{a} : \frac{\hat{b}'}{a'}.$$

It is evident that a cathetus can be lowered at any point of **a**, or of its extension. It is equally evident that each and any cathetus, related to the segment of base it intercepts, plays as one of two terms in the proportion which measures an identical angle $\frac{\hat{b}}{a}$.

This situation structures the concurrence of a factor of identity with a factor of indefinite variety, the former being the uniqueness of the angle concerned, the latter the absolute choice of the means of measure. In this conjunction of necessity and freedom, creative measure can be expressed.

NATURAL
NUMBER
IN
ANGLE
MEASURE

Provided

$$\frac{\hat{b}}{a} : \frac{\hat{b}'}{a'}$$

the *content* of **a**, **b**, **a**′, and **b**′ are left to absolute choice.

Placed within the scalar universe of geometry, this absolute choice, useless as such, is harnessed to **number**: given the angle $\frac{\hat{b}}{a}$, it is *not* indifferent where the cathetus is lowered, a useless choice. Within the absolute choice of number, the cathetus is lowered to *natural* number, so that it will be apparent that the indefinite series of natural number within which choice is absolute will be ordered in the measure of $\frac{\hat{b}}{a}$ as follows:

SIMILAR
TRIANGLES

$$\frac{\hat{b}}{a} : \frac{2\hat{b}}{2a} : \frac{3\hat{b}}{3a} : \frac{4\hat{b}}{4a} \cdots$$

Any two terms of the series are necessary and sufficient to the measure of $\frac{\hat{b}}{a}$.

In *practica*, the measure of $\frac{\hat{b}}{a}$ results in a series of triangular systems related by **similarity** (Figure 16).

INSCRIPTION
OF
SQUARE,
RECTANGLE,
AND
TRIANGLE

The isosceles* right triangle formed by the diagonal to the square is the first given triangle. A bisected square, it contains two right angles, one of which is evident, the other fractioned into the two acute angles which complete the isosceles right triangle (Figure 18a).

The side of a right triangle which faces the right angle is called hypotenuse.

As the diagonal to the square represents the particular case of unitary measure, so the hypotenuse of all fractional angle measures can be construed as diagonal to a rectangular figure (Figure 18b).

The intersection of both diagonals marks the center of a circle inscribing square and rectangle and consequently inscribing right triangles into a semicircle (Figure 18c). Within the construction of Figure 18c, there exists *sufficient* reason for all the inscribed triangles, one side of which is diameter of the inscribing circle, to be *right* triangles, as they were created by the diagonal of rectangular elements. Does *necessary* reason exist, without the construction of Figure 18c, for all angles inscribed on a diameter to be *right* angles? If, in Figure 18d, the identity of all diagonals is underlined by inscribed triangles constructed on one single diameter, it remains to be seen whether this diameter is a common hypotenuse.

For any angle whatsoever inscribed upon the diameter, Figure 18e shows OA = OP = OB, radius† of the inscribing semicircle, with OP partitioning the inscribed triangle into two isosceles triangles AOP and POB.

---

* From Greek "equal-legged," i.e., having two equal sides. A triangle having two equal sides evidently has two equal angles (Figure 17). The evidence is underlined by showing the equal sides as diagonals of equal rectangles (Figure 17a).

† $\dfrac{\text{radius}}{\text{diameter}} : \dfrac{1}{2}$

Figure 18e sustains the following argument:*

$$1)\ OA = OP \rightarrow \alpha = \alpha'$$

$$2)\ OP = OB \rightarrow \beta = \beta'$$

3) $\alpha + \alpha' + \beta + \beta' =$ two right angles
(sum of the angles of a triangle)

1) and 2)$\rightarrow$4) $2\alpha + 2\beta =$ two right angles

$$\alpha + \beta = \text{right angle}$$

hence $APB = \alpha + \beta = $ right angle.

In the isosceles right triangle formed by the diagonal to the square, the radius is perpendicular† to the diameter, by which attribute it forms two equal right triangles AOP and POB. There exists a mobility of the point P (guided by the semicircle APB and reined by the two hypotenuses AP and PB), exhausting the possibilities of right angles (Figure 19).

As the right angle APB semicircles, with AB a constant hypotenuse, there is a shift in the relation AQ : QP and QP : QB, shown in Figure 20 by two instances.‡

$$AQ' : Q'P',\ \ Q'P' : Q'B$$

and

$$AQ'' : Q''P'',\ Q''P'' : Q''B.$$

Constant in this figuration of two right triangles within a third, and valid for any position of P on the semicircle AB are the following facts:

1) All three triangles remain right triangles.

2) Each of the small right triangles has one acute angle in common with the large right triangle.

---

* The replacement symbol: "$\rightarrow$" is to be understood as implication.

† A perpendicular is the second side of a right angle. When a right angle is drawn, a line is drawn first and the second side forming the right angle must be perpendicular to fulfill its function. The geometric grid can be viewed as a structure of perpendiculars.

‡ Although precision of geometric nomenclature lies in its form, not its substance, there is a benefit of recognition in a consistent choice of names. Thus **O** is reserved for the center of a circle, actual or potential, **Q** is always mean term between **A** and **B**, while **P** stands for a point in its most generally accepted usage, be it on a circle or as the fixed end of a vibrating string.

This constitutes sufficient reason for similarity within right triangles.

In the inscribed right triangle APB, the altitude PQ, perpendicular to AB, divides the triangle APB into two right triangles AQP and PQB so that

AQP is similar to APB

and PQB is similar to APB;

hence AQP is similar to PQB.

(Figure 21a).

The right triangle PQB can be rotated around Q and P and made to coincide with A, showing the angular measure

$$\frac{b}{a} : \frac{b'}{a'} \qquad \text{(Figure 21b)}$$

where

$$b = QB$$
$$a = QP$$
$$b' = QP$$
$$a' = QA$$

so that $\dfrac{QB}{QP} : \dfrac{QP}{QA}$, a geometric proportion.

This theorem, attributed to Thales, shows that any perpendicular lowered from a semicircle onto the diameter constitutes the mean term of a geometric proportion and divides the diameter into two segments which are the extremes of the proportion.*

---

* In Figure 21a it can also be shown

that $\alpha + \beta' =$ right angle
and $\alpha + \beta \ =$ right angle
so that $\beta = \beta'$
and $\alpha = \alpha'$.

PROPORTIONAL RELATIONS WITHIN TRIANGLE
INSCRIBED IN SEMICIRCLE AND ITS CATHETUS

In Figure 21a, all three right triangles are similar:

$$\frac{\text{cathetus}}{\text{hypotenuse}} = \frac{PB}{AB} : \frac{PQ}{AP} \rightarrow \frac{PB}{PQ} : \frac{AB}{AP}$$

$$PQ \times AB = PB \times AP$$

$$\boxed{PQ = \frac{PB \times AP}{AB}}$$

$$\frac{\text{base}}{\text{hypotenuse}} = \frac{AQ}{AP} : \frac{AP}{AB} \rightarrow \boxed{AQ = \frac{(AP)^2}{AB}}$$

$$\frac{\text{cathetus}}{\text{hypotenuse}} = \frac{QB}{PB} : \frac{PB}{AB} \rightarrow \boxed{QB = \frac{(PB)^2}{AB}.}$$

If the diameter of the inscribing circle is considered as 1 :

$$AB = 1 \rightarrow PQ = PB \times AP$$
$$AQ = (AP)^2$$
$$QB = (PB)^2.$$

RATIONAL ANGLES

Rational angles are such that they are measurable by their sole situation on the geometric grid. In a rational angle, the base always lies on the grid while its diagonal side is hypotenuse to the right angle formed by the grid. Additions and subtractions of rational angles are rational in their sums and remainders.[*]

Two angles to be added are first constructed on a common basis, for example

$$\frac{b}{a} + \frac{d}{c} = \frac{\overset{\wedge}{2}}{5} + \frac{\overset{\wedge}{1}}{4} = \frac{\overset{\wedge}{8}}{20} + \frac{\overset{\wedge}{5}}{20} \qquad \text{(Figure 22)}.$$

The smaller angle is then constructed upon the hypotenuse of the larger one and the cathetus of the total angle lowered upon the base (Figure 22a). As the grid shows, the sum of the two angles is $\frac{\overset{\wedge}{13}}{18}$, so that in general terms:

$$\frac{\hat{b}}{a} + \frac{\hat{d}}{c} = \frac{\overset{\frown}{bc + ad}}{ac - bd}.$$

In order to subtract one angle from another, a common base for the two angles must again be found. On this common base, the larger angle is constructed, and its hypotenuse will serve as base for the smaller angle to be deducted (Figure 22b). In general terms:

$$\frac{\hat{b}}{a} - \frac{\hat{d}}{c} = \frac{\overset{\frown}{bc - ad}}{ac + bd}.$$

---

[*] R.A. Schwaller de Lubicz treats angles in proportional notation and their manipulation (*Temple de l'Homme* I, 297 ff., 306 ff.), but these angles cease to be rational in sums and remainders so that general formulas for addition and subtraction can be elucidated only through auxiliary grids and are not *evident* through the practice of the figuration. Figures 22a and 22b aim to contribute this evidence to de Lubicz's basic work in Pharaonic trigonometry.

DIMIDIATION OF ANGLES

Given $\dfrac{\hat{b}}{a}$, $\dfrac{\hat{y}}{x}$ exists so that

$$\frac{\hat{y}}{x} + \frac{\hat{y}}{x} = \frac{\hat{b}}{a}$$

$$\frac{\hat{y}}{x} + \frac{\hat{y}}{x} = \frac{yx + yx}{x^2 - y^2} = \frac{2yx}{x^2 - y^2} = \frac{\hat{b}}{a}.$$

Assuming $y = \mathbf{b}$*

$$\text{If } y = b, \frac{2bx}{x^2 - b^2} = \frac{\hat{b}}{a}$$

$\longrightarrow$ $a\,(2\,bx) = b(x^2 - b^2)$
$\longrightarrow$ $2\,ax = x^2 - b^2$
$\longrightarrow$ $x^2 - 2\,ax = b^2$
$\longrightarrow$ $(x^2 - 2ax + a^2) - a^2 = b^2$
$\longrightarrow$ $(x - a)^2 = b^2 + a^2$
$\longrightarrow$ $x - a = \sqrt{b^2 + a^2}$

$\longrightarrow$ $\boxed{x = \sqrt{b^2 + a^2} + a}$ (Figure 23)

Conclusion: To dimidiate a given angle $\dfrac{\hat{b}}{a}$, the hypotenuse $\sqrt{a^2 + b^2}$ is added to the base $\mathbf{a}$ and the cathetus $y = \mathbf{b}$ of the dimidiating angle is raised on the total base $\sqrt{a^2 + b^2} + \mathbf{a}$.

---

* The cathetus $\mathbf{y}$ of the unknown angle may be raised at any point on $\mathbf{x}$ provided $\mathbf{x} > \mathbf{a}$. By choosing $y = \mathbf{b}$, one unknown is eliminated, and calculation of $\mathbf{x}$ becomes possible.

THEOREM OF PYTHAGORAS

To prove: $a^2 + b^2 = c^2$

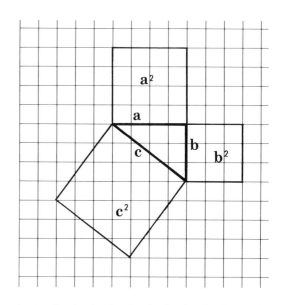

KLMN $= (a + b)^2$
      $= a^2 + 2ab + b^2.$

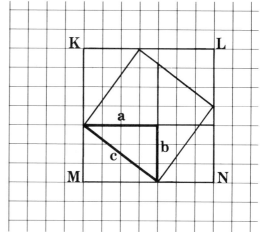

The large square KLMN consists of: $a^2 + b^2 + 2ab$
and
the large square KLMN consists of: $c^2 + 4 \left(\dfrac{ab}{2} \right)$

hence: $a^2 + b^2 + 2ab = c^2 + 4 \left(\dfrac{ab}{2} \right)$

$a^2 + b^2 + \cancel{2ab} = c^2 + \cancel{2ab}$

$$\boxed{a^2 + b^2 = c^2.}$$

CYCLICAL ASPECT OF HARMONY AND GEOMETRIC PROGRESSION

The basic principle of vibrating strings can be observed on the monochord. As the stop is moved to decrease the string length, the rate of vibration increases along with the pitch ("height") of the note sounded. Precise observation records that if the string is *halved*, the rate of vibration is *doubled*. The relation between string length and vibration is termed **inverse**.

If the string is plucked and the stop is slowly moved toward the center of the string, the pitch of the original tone will rise until it reaches, at precisely half the length of the original string, a tone so closely duplicating the original fundamental tone that intuition unquestioningly perceives the end point of a cycle. If the fundamental tone of the entire string were called C_1, then the tone of half the string is best termed C_2.

If furthermore the fundamental tone C_1 vibrates at 1 vibration per unit of time, then C_2 vibrates at 2 vibrations per unit of time. Thus the following table can be established:

NOTE	STRING LENGTH	VIBRATION
C_1	1	1
C_2	½	2

This situation is represented by the circle-diameter and can be shown on the monochord:

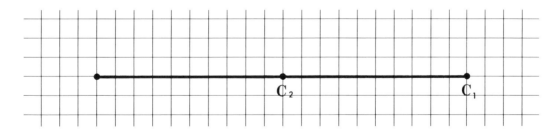

The vibrating part of the string lies to the left of the symbol (the entire string for C_1, one half the string for C_2).

It is evident that by halving again the string length ½ which produces C_2, a tone will be found standing in relation to C_2 as C_2 stood to C_1, namely as a second partial if C_2 is considered as fundamental or first partial. This tone can be called C_3 and described as follows:

NOTE	STRING LENGTH	VIBRATION
C_3	$\dfrac{1}{4}$	4

As this tone is produced by the string C_1 vibrating at ¼ its length, C_3 also constitutes the 4th partial of C_1.

Continuing the dichotomy, the next tone produced will be:

NOTE	STRING LENGTH	VIBRATION
C_4	$\dfrac{1}{8}$	8

which will be the 8th partial of C_1, and further

C_5	$\dfrac{1}{16}$	16

which will be the 16th partial of C_1.

We readily see that a geometric series is thus produced:

$$1, 2, 4, 8, 16, \ldots$$

as

$$C_1/C_2 : C_2/C_3 : C_3/C_4 : C_4/C_5,$$

or in vibrations:

$$\frac{1}{2} : \frac{2}{4} : \frac{4}{8} : \frac{8}{16}$$

It is sufficient to harmony to study the measure of the distance between 1 and 2, knowing that the distances between 2 and 4, 4 and 8, 8 and 16, would yield no different measure, but only a different scale. As all these measures would be proportionate, they could all be reduced to the measure of the distance of the first dichotomy. Derived from a geometric scission of unity through the diagonal of the square, the study of this phenomenon properly belongs to geometry.

The square and its diagonal shown as square form the geometric scission of unity leading to a proliferation of number. The scission of unity through the root of duality and the resultant duality are shown in *practica* and thus appear as surfaces (Figure 9). The proportionate measure is a syntactic of terms and a part of *theoria*. It does not appear in *practica*.*

The geometric mean term measuring the distance between 1 and 2 is the root of 2 and leads to the expression

$$\frac{1}{\sqrt{2}} \; : \; \frac{\sqrt{2}}{2}$$

which is a geometric proportion. This proportion exemplifies the function of mean terms in general. Indeed, the diagonal of the square pertains to the square as its diagonal and as such it functions inside unity, the square 1. But it is also the root of 2, the side of square 2, and has thus a relationship with the extreme term.**

---

* This reflects the incapacity of the eye to receive proportionate measure. The ear is remarkable for being the only sensory organ capable of judging proportion. It detects *exact* string ratios such as ½, ⅔, ¾, and thus is capable of determining intervals basic to harmonic proportionate measure.

** True contemplation of Figure 9 reveals a double image, depending on whether the figure is viewed as a scission of unity, or as duality "held together on four sides," i.e., defined by four approaches. Both extremes being related to the mean, the latter term appears as the relation between extreme terms.

The essence of the geometric proportion lies in the identical relation of root to diagonal in any and all squares. In the square of which the root is 1, the relation reads $\dfrac{1}{\sqrt{2}}$, in the square of which the root is 2, it will read $\dfrac{2}{2\sqrt{2}}$, and if the root be 3, $\dfrac{3}{3\sqrt{2}}$, etc. In the present example where the square is 2, its root is $\sqrt{2}$, and the relation of root to diagonal reads:

$$\frac{\sqrt{2}}{\sqrt{2}\sqrt{2}} \to \frac{\sqrt{2}}{2}.$$

In all cases, the diagonal is $\sqrt{2}$, a function perfectly represented.

Bisecting or halving the string produces a duplication of the fundamental tone and the second partial. In striking the distance between 1 and 2 as C_1 and C_2, the node* marks the limit of harmonic study. All consequent harmonic events can be referred to the dual expression of this interval as string length (in the distance 1 to ½) or as vibrations (in the distance 1 to 2).

The third partial depends on the trisection of the string. As the circle represents a fundamental tone or first partial, its diameter is instrumental in determining a second partial. A third partial will be a function of the inscribed triangle which in turn is dependent upon the radius or half diameter (Figure 24).

As the string length of the third partial is 1/3 and as it vibrates at the rate of 3 vibrations per unit of time, it falls outside the limit of study:

$$\text{in string length:} \quad \frac{1}{3} \; < \; \frac{1}{2} \; < \; 1$$

$$\underbrace{\phantom{\frac{1}{2} \; < \; 1}}_{\text{HARMONY}}$$

$$\text{in vibrations:} \quad 3 \; > \; 2 \; > \; 1.$$

$$\underbrace{}_{\text{HARMONY}}$$

---

* Nodes and harmonic representations: Nodes are motionless points on a vibrating string, occurring as the natural phenomenon productive of overtones (when nodes segment the string in the manner exposed above) or else when the vibratory medium is mechanically stopped at any point along its dimension. The string is perfectly represented within the scalar universe of geometry by a line on which nodes can be shown as points. Only artificially produced nodes need be indicated, the position of natural nodes being always implied, but irrelevant unless indexed by a nodal point on the linear representation. The extremities of the line representing the vibrating string will be marked by two nodal points, and it is evident that a third point fingered between these extremes will in fact cause the single system to be superseded by two strings capable of vibrating independently. The stopped string differs from a system of natural nodes in that the latter retains the fundamental while sounding its harmonics, whereas the former gives two new fundamentals (and their harmonics), one on each side of the third nodal point.

It will be the rule of harmonic representation to name a tone by its conventional letter written beneath the node determining its string length. Unless otherwise indicated, strings will be shortened from right to left, so that the extreme left node is fixed. Only the segment situated between the fixed left and the movable node designating the tone under study will be considered to be vibrating.

The third partial can be duplicated, however, as has been done for C_1, by doubling the string length, thus halving the vibrations. If the third partial is termed G, its duplicate can be termed G_1 and inserted between C_1 and C_2:

Note	String Length	Vibration
G	$\dfrac{1}{3}$	3
G_1	$\dfrac{2}{3}$	$\dfrac{3}{2}$

in string length: $\quad \dfrac{1}{2} < \dfrac{2}{3} < 1$

$$\underbrace{\qquad\qquad}_{\text{HARMONY}}$$

in vibrations: $\quad 2 > \dfrac{3}{2} > 1.$

$$\underbrace{\qquad\qquad}_{\text{HARMONY}}$$

In Table III, relative string length and vibration have been expressed in whole numbers.

Examination shows that $C_2 - G_1 - C_1$ progress harmonically when expressed as string length:

$$\frac{4-3}{3} : \frac{6-4}{6} = \frac{1}{3}.$$

They progress arithmetically when expressed as vibrations:

$$4 - 3 = 3 - 2 = 1.$$

The distance of one to two is traversed by two progressions, arithmetic and harmonic. Measured in *vibrations*, the distance between C_1 and C_2 is the distance between one and two.

Measured in *string length*, C_1 to C_2 is the distance between 1 and ½, the inverse of the vibrational measure.

The *distance* measured by vibration is identical to the *distance* measured in string length.

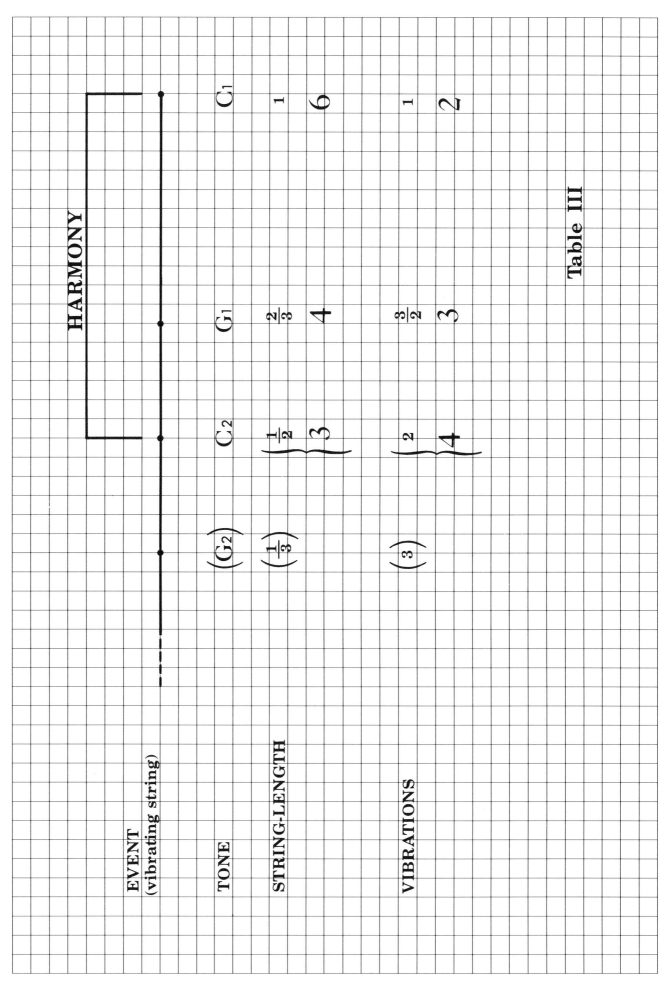

EVENT (vibrating string)			
TONE	C_1	G_1	C_2	(G_2)
STRING-LENGTH	1	$\frac{2}{3}$	$\frac{1}{2}$	$\left(\frac{1}{3}\right)$
	6	4	3	
VIBRATIONS	1	$\frac{3}{2}$	2	(3)
	2	3	4	

HARMONY

Table III

56

The *measures*, however, are the inverse one to the other.*

The two progressions are necessary and sufficient to a definitive measure of the distance between one and two.

They afford a proportional measure with two mean terms, one drawn from each progression, termed **musical proportion** by Nicomachus of Gerasa (1st century A.D.), a neo-Pythagorean of Arabic descent.

Combining both progressions on the basis of the arithmetic progression $C_1 - G_1 - C_2$ (vibrations), or $2 - 3 - 4$, the harmonic mean between 2 and 4. is interjected:

$$\text{Harmonic mean:} \qquad 2 - q - 4$$

$$(2 + 4)q = 2 \cdot 2 \cdot 4$$

$$6q = 16$$

$$q = 8/3$$

$$\text{Musical proportion:} \quad 2 - 8/3 - 3 - 4$$

$$\text{In whole numbers:} \quad 6 - 8 - 9 - 12.$$

Combining both progressions on the basis of the harmonic progression $C_1 - G_1 - C_2$ (string length) or $6 - 4 - 3$, the arithmetic mean between 6 and 3 is interjected:

$$\text{Arithmetic mean:} \qquad \frac{6 + 3}{2} = \frac{9}{2}$$

$$\text{Musical proportion:} \quad 6 - 9/2 - 4 - 3$$

$$\text{In whole numbers:} \quad 12 - 9 - 8 - 6.$$

---

* If $\quad \mathbf{b} < \mathbf{q} < \mathbf{a} \quad$ progress harmonically,

$$\text{then } \frac{2ab}{a+b} = q.$$

If $\quad \dfrac{1}{\mathbf{b}} > \dfrac{1}{\mathbf{q}} > \dfrac{1}{\mathbf{a}} \quad$ progress arithmetically,

$$\text{then } \frac{\dfrac{1}{b} + \dfrac{1}{a}}{2} \rightarrow \frac{\dfrac{b + a}{ab}}{2} \rightarrow \frac{b + a}{2ab} = q.$$

The terms of the musical proportion are the same in both approaches, only the order of terms is reversed.*

The second mean term interpolated in the above development is conventionally designated as F.

Note	String Length	Vibrations
C_1	1	1
F_1	3/4	4/3
G_1	2/3	3/2
C_2	1/2	2

The musical proportion is the fundamental expression in harmony of the most general proportionate measure, the four-term proportion:

$$\frac{b}{a} : \frac{d}{c} \rightarrow \frac{b}{d} : \frac{a}{c}.$$

In harmony:
$$\frac{C_1}{G_1} : \frac{F_1}{C_2} \rightarrow \frac{C_1}{F_1} : \frac{G_1}{C_2}$$

is the measure of two distances known respectively as:

the interval of fifths:
$$\frac{C_1}{G_1} : \frac{F_1}{C_2}$$

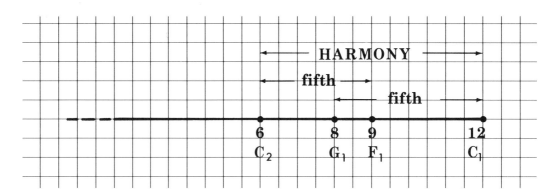

---

*Although as a general rule the string is read from right to left (with P as a fixed point on the extreme left of the string), the reversal of direction forced by the inverse points of view of vibration and string length necessitates the contemplation of harmonic events from left to right on the string as well (as if P′ were a fixed point on the extreme *right* of the string). The latter reading will be considered as a reversed polarity of the string.

the interval of fourths:

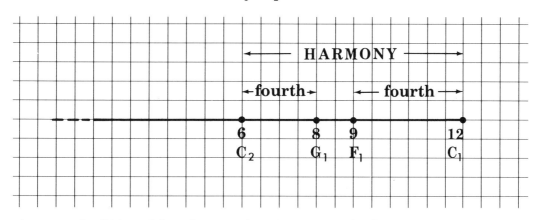

$$\frac{C_1}{F_1} : \frac{G_1}{C_2}$$

The sum of a fifth and fourth comprises the octave, the field of harmony.

MEASURE OF OCTAVE BY
MUSICAL PROPORTION

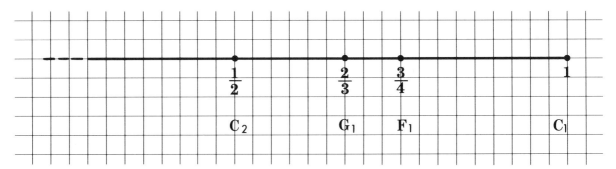

	NUMBER			DISTANCE	TONE			INTERVAL
	$\frac{6}{9}$	:	$\frac{8}{12}$	$= \frac{2}{3}$	$\frac{C_1}{F}$	:	$\frac{G}{C}$	$=$ fifth
STRING LENGTH								
	$\frac{6}{8}$	:	$\frac{9}{12}$	$= \frac{3}{4}$	$\frac{C_1}{G}$	:	$\frac{F}{C}$	$=$ fourth
	$\frac{9}{6}$	:	$\frac{12}{8}$	$= \frac{3}{2}$	$\frac{F}{C_1}$	:	$\frac{C}{G}$	$=$ fifth
VIBRATIONS								
	$\frac{8}{6}$	:	$\frac{12}{9}$	$= \frac{4}{3}$	$\frac{G}{C_1}$	:	$\frac{C}{F}$	$=$ fourth

	DISTANCE	INTERVAL
STRING LENGTH	$\frac{2}{3} \times \frac{3}{4} = \frac{1}{2}$	fifth + fourth = octave
VIBRATIONS	$\frac{3}{2} \times \frac{4}{3} = 2$	fifth + fourth = octave

The fourth partial with nodes at 1/4, 1/2, 3/4 string length determines C_3. By the 3/4 string length which it produces, it furthermore implies F_1 more directly than any other partial of C.

It is beyond our present scope to examine the set of regular polygons which can be constructed with compass and ruler and the relation of these inscribed polygons to the elements of harmony. This topic attracted Johannes Kepler's attention in his "Harmonices Mundi" (1619), and a clear discussion of the question can be found in Max Caspar's "Kepler."* The problem of the internal intervals of the octave was solved by equal temperament only for keyboard instruments in Western music; the series of overtones certainly does not furnish a ready-made answer. As shown by Kepler, only polygons which can be constructed with the help of straight lines and circles need be considered, which indicates an inherent compatibility of harmonic and geometric constitutions. Even within these limits, Kepler finds exceptions and a need for further conditioning.

Studies abound on the inscribed pentagon which determines a string length 1/5 and corresponds to the fifth partial. It suffices to underline the remarkable causal chain from ϕ to the root of five and to the expression of the number five in the regular pentagon. Harmonically, the string length 1/5 must be doubled twice before it takes its place within the octave as string length 4/5 with the conventional designation of E. The first five partials suffice for the vibrating string clearly to sound the major triad C-E-G, the cornerstone of tonality.

---

* Max Caspar, *Kepler*, (Abelard-Schuman 1959), pp. 264 et seq.

Φ BY SURFACES

When unity dichotomizes into unequal parts in such a manner that the sum of the two fractions equals the whole or unity, the one and only measure expressive of this dichotomy will read:

$$\frac{c}{b} : \frac{b}{1} = \phi$$

where $c < b$

$c + b = 1$

$c = b^2.$

The above is a particular case of a more general proportion called geometric:

$$\frac{c}{b} : \frac{b}{a}$$

where $c < b < a$

$c + b \neq a$

$ac = b^2.$

Both the above expressions denote geometric events through the geometric element b^2. The square by its root gives a standing to **b** (Figure 25a), and by its diagonal **b** $\sqrt{2}$, the semicircular housing of a geometric proportion to the expression

$$\frac{c}{b} : \frac{b}{a} \qquad \text{(Figure 25b)}.$$

Figure 25b analyzes into

$$\frac{c}{b} : \frac{b}{2b + c}$$

showing $a = c + 2b$ (Figure 25c)

whereas unity dichotomizes into the condition

$$a = c + b = 1.$$

It is intuitively clear that a progression from the constitution of **a** as (**c** + 2**b**) to **a** as (**c** + **b**) is a diminution of **b** to a point $\frac{b}{2}$, and that the inscribing housing for a ϕ proportion is swung by a semi-diagonal (sd) from that point (Figure 25d).

If the function creative of the geometric proportion in Figure 25b is named $\sqrt{2}$, what specific name is expressive of the creative function ϕ in Figure 25d? The function creates the expression which gives rise to number, and only through number can the function be specifically named.

The diagonal to the square reveals its name when the square is unity.

The semi-diagonal (sd) under similar conditions yields:

$$1^2 + \left(\frac{1}{2}\right)^2 = (sd)^2 = 1 + \frac{1}{4} = \frac{5}{4}$$

$$sd = \frac{\sqrt{5}}{2}.$$

The function ϕ is directly creative of the root of five (Figures 25e and f).

The geometric proportion $\frac{c}{b} : \frac{b}{a}$ transforms a square into a rectangle:

$$\frac{c}{b} : \frac{b}{a} \longrightarrow b^2 = ac \qquad \text{(Figure 25g)}.$$

ϕ transforms a square into a rectangle plus a square:

$$\frac{c}{b} : \frac{b}{c+b} \longrightarrow b^2 = cb + c^2 \qquad \text{(Figure 25h)}.$$

If in the foregoing discussion of ϕ, the condition of

$$a = c + b$$

has been met, not so the further condition of

$$c + b = 1.$$

It is manifest, however, that if

$$c + b = 1$$

then both **c** and **b** must be fractions of unity.

As ϕ converts a square into the sum of a rectangle and a square, it expresses itself within unity as

$$\frac{1}{\phi} + \frac{1}{\phi^2} = 1 \qquad \text{(Figure 25i)}.$$

All relations of ϕ and its powers have geometric existence as surfaces and can now be evolved.

In Figure 25i, the rectangle $\frac{1}{\phi} + \frac{1}{\phi^2} = 1$.

As one side of this rectangle is known to be $\frac{1}{\phi}$, the long side must be ϕ, so that

$$\frac{1}{\phi} \times \phi = 1 \qquad \text{(Figure 25j)}$$

Considering next the vertical rectangle formed by 1^2 added to the horizontal rectangle $\frac{1}{\phi}$, its large side is ϕ, its small side is 1, so that the value of the rectangle is ϕ (Figure 25k). The figure also shows

$$\phi + \frac{1}{\phi^2} = 2.$$

ϕ^2 can now be completed (Figure 25l):

$$\phi^2 = 1 + 2\left(\frac{1}{\phi}\right) + \frac{1}{\phi^2} = \left(1 + \frac{1}{\phi}\right)^2.$$

It is known that $\qquad 1 + \frac{1}{\phi} = \phi \qquad \text{(Figure 25k)}$

$\qquad\qquad$ and $\qquad \frac{1}{\phi} + \frac{1}{\phi^2} = 1 \qquad \text{(Figure 25j)}$

Hence, in ϕ^2

$$\phi + 1 = \phi^2$$

$\qquad\qquad$ and $\qquad \frac{2}{\phi} + \frac{1}{\phi^2} = \phi \qquad \text{(Figures 25m and n)}.$

GEOMETRIC MEASURE AND
HARMONIC PROPORTION

In geometric practice, a proportionate angular measure is expressed by similar triangles (Figure 26a). The angular measure

$$\frac{b}{a} : \frac{b'}{a'}$$

expresses a four-term proportion

$$\frac{b}{a} : \frac{d}{c}$$

which can be explicated by an outward projection of the smaller component of the angle measure, thus forming the geometric figuration of four-term proportions (Figure 26b) where

$$\frac{b}{a} : \frac{b'}{a'}$$

implying

$$\frac{b}{b'} : \frac{a}{a'}$$

in the particular case where

$$a' = 3a$$
$$b' = 3b.$$

The latter implication is apparent when it is remembered that any $\frac{b'}{a'}$ is a multiple of $\frac{b}{a}$ from the series

$$\frac{b}{a} : \frac{2b}{2a} : \frac{3b}{3a} : \frac{4b}{4a} \cdots$$

so that the integers forming the relation $\dfrac{b}{b'}$ are identical to those forming $\dfrac{a}{a'}$ once the relation has been simplified by b or a respectively, for example

$$\frac{2b}{4b} : \frac{2a}{4a} \longrightarrow \frac{2}{4} : \frac{2}{4}.$$

The definition of harmonic proportion

$$\frac{q-b}{b} : \frac{a-q}{a}$$

is an expression of the four-term proportion

$$\frac{n}{m} : \frac{n'}{m'}$$

All harmonic proportions can thus be transformed into an angular measure expressed by

$$\frac{\hat{n}}{m}.$$

If the angle measure is opposed horizontally (Figure 26c), a first step is taken toward the geometric representation of the harmonic proportion. If indeed the horizontal line is seen as the segment BA of a vibrating string PA, a node Q is given which relates $\dfrac{QB}{QA}$, the first relation in the harmonic measure $\dfrac{QB}{QA} : \dfrac{PB}{PA}$.

P is the unknown fixed point of the vibrating string, and its position can be geometrically located (Figure 26d). For it is known that

$$\frac{QB}{QA} : \frac{BB'}{AA'}$$

and the verticals BB' and AA' can be construed as the two catheti of an angle measure

$$\frac{\overset{\wedge}{AA'}}{PA} : \frac{\overset{\wedge}{BB'}}{PB}$$

at a point P, the projected intersection of $A'B'$ with AB.

On the other hand,

$$\frac{QB}{QA} : \frac{BB'}{AA'}$$

so that

$$\frac{BB'}{AA'} : \frac{QB}{QA} : \frac{PB}{PA}$$

and in

$$\frac{QB}{QA} : \frac{PB}{PA}$$

can be found the measure of an harmonic proportion (Figure 26e).

The geometric figuration of the harmonic proportion thus consists of three interrelated elements:

1. an angular measure $\frac{b}{a} : \frac{b'}{a'}$

2. a four-term proportion $\frac{b}{QB} : \frac{b'}{QA}$

3. a vibrating string **PA** with two internal nodes **B** and **Q** so that

$$\frac{PB}{PA} : \frac{QB}{QA}.$$

HARMONIC STRING LENGTH

For Philosophical Geometry, an harmonic progression exists as a series of nodes on a vibrating string. As such, its representation is a segment of circle stretched between an extreme fixed point **P** on the left and an extreme movable node **A** to the right. Thus if in theory $b < q < a$ progress harmonically, then in practice

$$PB < PQ < PA.$$

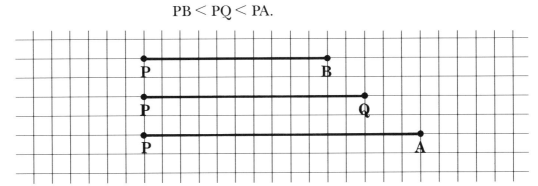

Whereas in *theoria*, the harmonic measure between two terms **a** and **b** can be shown by means of those two extremes to reside in a mean term

$$\frac{2ab}{a + b},$$

in *practica*, four nodes are providing the intervals **PA, PQ, PB** as three different string lengths, **PA** being the unitary string while the small length **PB** as well as the mean length **PQ** are fractions thereof.

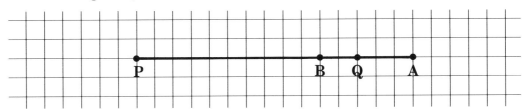

In theory, then, it is possible to establish harmonic proportions between any two terms $b < a$ by means of $\frac{2ab}{a + b} = q$, yet such a fractional expression cannot be translated into a string length **PQ** and thus has no practical existence. In order to achieve geometric existence in whole numbers, the three theoretical terms of the harmonic proportion $(b < \frac{2ab}{a + b} < a)$ are multiplied by $(a + b)$, yielding

$$b(a + b) < 2ab < a(a + b)$$

or
$$ab + a^2 = PB$$

$$2ab = PQ$$

$$a^2 + ab = PA.$$

In the harmonic measure of the distance between 1 and 2, the extreme terms of the proportion were $\mathbf{b} = 1$

$$\mathbf{a} = 2$$

hence

$$PB = ab + b^2 = 2 + 1^2 = 3$$

$$PQ = 2ab = 2 \bullet 1 \bullet 2 = 4$$

$$PA = a^2 + ab = 4 + 2 = 6$$

where

	String Length	Vibrations
PA = 6	1	1
PQ = 4	2/3	3/2
PB = 3	1/2	2

showing the scalar string lengths as an harmonic progression $3 - 4 - 6$ in its relation to the third partial.

A direct polarity is imposed upon the string by assigning the fixed point **P** to its one extreme, the movable point **A** to the other. While the harmonic measure progresses with a necessary movement from **P** to **A**, it is given *direction* only by the fortuitous assignment of **P** to one extreme, **A** to the other. This factor of contingency is neutralized by reversing polarities and studying the string under both direct and reversed polarities.

Direct polarity exists if **P** is the left extreme, **A** the right:

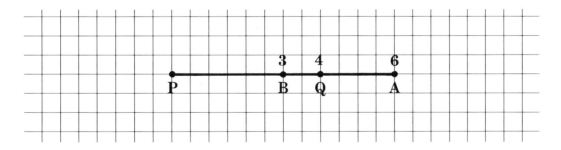

Reversed polarity shows the harmonic progression of the third partial determining another node at string length 1/3:

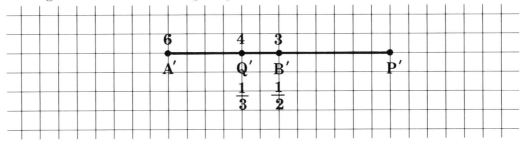

Considered under both polarities, the string shows three nodes (beside the extremes) with **PB** = **P′B′**, so that **B** and **B′** coincide:

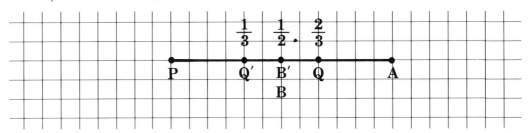

It is remarkable that the harmonic points determined in reverse polarity give rise in direct polarity to another harmonic progression where

$$PB = 2, \quad PQ = 3, \quad PA = 6$$

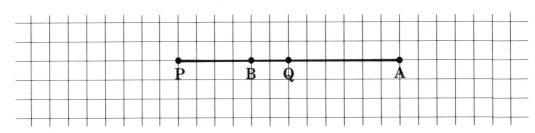

and

$$\frac{PB}{PA} : \frac{QB}{QA}, \quad \frac{b}{a} : \frac{1}{3}$$

as

$$\frac{3-2}{2} : \frac{6-3}{6} = \frac{1}{2} = \frac{n}{m}.$$

The foregoing furnishes evidence of an indefinite number of string lengths **PA** each accommodating on the geometric grid a pair of harmonic proportions related by their expression of an identical harmonic reading in direct and reverse polarity. Each pair comprises an upper and a lower proportion depending on the proximity of **q** to **b** or to **a** respectively. In these terms, and on the basis of a string length 15, for example, 3 − 5 − 15 is the lower, 10 − 12 − 15 the upper proportion. In general terms, lower proportions are designated by the letters **b** < **q** < **a**, upper proportions by their primes **b′** < **q′** < **a′**.

Full coherence in geometric harmony is achieved only by deriving harmonic proportion from angle measure (Figures 26a to e); with an initial datum of $\overset{\wedge}{\dfrac{b}{a}}$, the perpendicular **AA′**, usually considered a mere mechanism of measure (its magnitude being irrelevant to its framing function), is reduced to a multiple **m** of $\overset{\wedge}{\dfrac{b}{a}}$*. With $\overset{\wedge}{\dfrac{b}{a}}$ as a first element, $\dfrac{n}{m}$ is readily determined as $\dfrac{a-b}{a+b}$ and

$$q = b + \frac{n}{m}\,b = a - \frac{n}{m}\,a$$

where fractions are eliminated by multiplying by **m**

$$mq = mb + nb = ma - na,$$

an expression shown on the grid as

$$PQ = PB + QB = PA - QA.$$

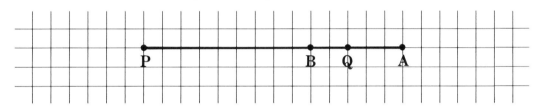

In deriving an harmonic proportion from a sole angle measure, it must be kept in mind that for any angle $\overset{\wedge}{\dfrac{b}{a}}$ there exists an indefinite number of angles $\overset{\wedge}{\dfrac{b}{a}}{}' : \overset{\wedge}{\dfrac{b}{a}}{}'' : \overset{\wedge}{\dfrac{b}{a}}{}''' \cdots = \overset{\wedge}{\dfrac{b}{a}}$ (Figure 16) which the geometric grid identifies with the series of natural numbers

$$\overset{\wedge}{\frac{1b}{1a}} : \overset{\wedge}{\frac{2b}{2a}} : \overset{\wedge}{\frac{3b}{3a}} : \overset{\wedge}{\frac{4b}{4a}} \cdots = \overset{\wedge}{\frac{b}{a}}.$$

For every angle $\overset{\wedge}{\dfrac{b}{a}}$, there exist two angles

$$\overset{\wedge}{\frac{nb}{na}} : \overset{\wedge}{\frac{mb}{ma}} = \overset{\wedge}{\frac{b}{a}}$$

---

* This basic procedure in the addition of equal angles led R.A. Schwaller de Lubicz to the superb Pharaonic synthesis of the "Bolt" ("Le Verrou," *Temple de L'Homme,* Vol. I, page 309).

where $m > n$, and such that $mb + nb = ma - na$ (Figure 27) whence

$$b(m + n) = a(m - n)$$

$$\rightarrow \frac{b}{a} = \frac{m - n}{m + n}$$

and q is the point where

$$na + nb = ma - mb$$

$$\rightarrow n(a + b) = m(a - b)$$

$$\rightarrow \frac{n}{m} = \frac{a - b}{a + b}.$$

Table IV

HARMONIC PROPORTIONS ON THE SEVEN SHORTEST STRING LENGTHS

String ($a \times m$)	H. P.	$\dfrac{\hat{b}}{a}$	+	$\dfrac{\hat{n}}{m}$	=	$\dfrac{1}{1}$	$\dfrac{a + b}{2}$	$\dfrac{q}{a}$
6	2-3-6	1/3		1/2			4	1/2
	3-4-6	1/2		1/3		$\dfrac{5}{5}$	9/2	2/3
15	3-5-15	1/5		2/3			9	1/3
	10-12-15	2/3		1/5		$\dfrac{13}{13}$	25/2	4/5
20	5-8-20	1/4		3/5			25/2	2/5
	12-15-20	3/5		1/4		$\dfrac{17}{17}$	16	3/4
28	4-7-28	1/7		3/4			16	1/4
	21-24-28	3/4		1/7		$\dfrac{25}{25}$	49/2	6/7
35	14-20-35	2/5		3/7			49/2	4/7
	15-21-35	3/7		2/5		$\dfrac{29}{29}$	25	3/5
42	7-12-42	1/6		5/7			49/2	2/7
	30-35-42	5/7		1/6		$\dfrac{37}{37}$	36	5/6
45	5-9-45	1/9		4/5			25	1/5
	36-40-45	4/5		1/9		$\dfrac{41}{41}$	81/2	8/9

COMMENT ON TABLE IV

The Table analyzes the seven shortest string lengths that afford a geometric interpretation on the grid. Figure 28 exemplifies such harmonic string lengths by showing for string length 20 the lower and upper proportions combined into an expression of both around the common diagonal. The latter is the very index of harmonic measure, being always diagonal to a square, in other words, hypotenuse to $\dfrac{\overset{\wedge}{1}}{1}$.

Rational angles show the complementary relation of

$$\frac{\hat{b}}{a} + \frac{\hat{n}}{m} = \overset{\wedge}{1}\,.$$

If an arithmetic proportion is injected into each harmonic proportion, forming a series of pseudo-musical proportions, $\dfrac{\mathbf{a + b}}{2}$ in each case will be a square or half a square.

THE FIGURES

Figure 0

Figure 1

Figure 2

Figure 3

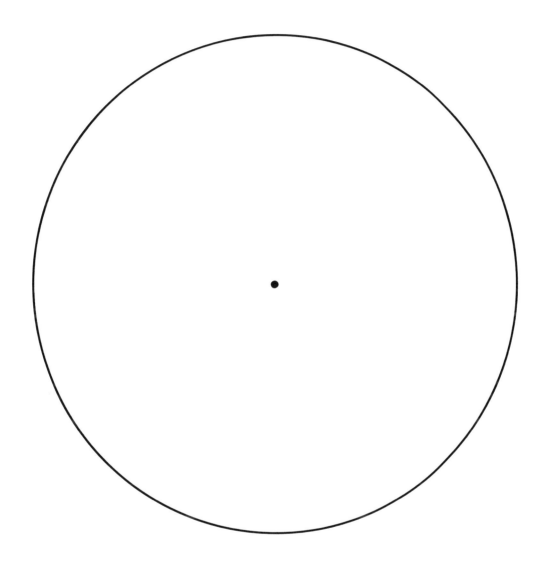

Figure 4

Figure 5

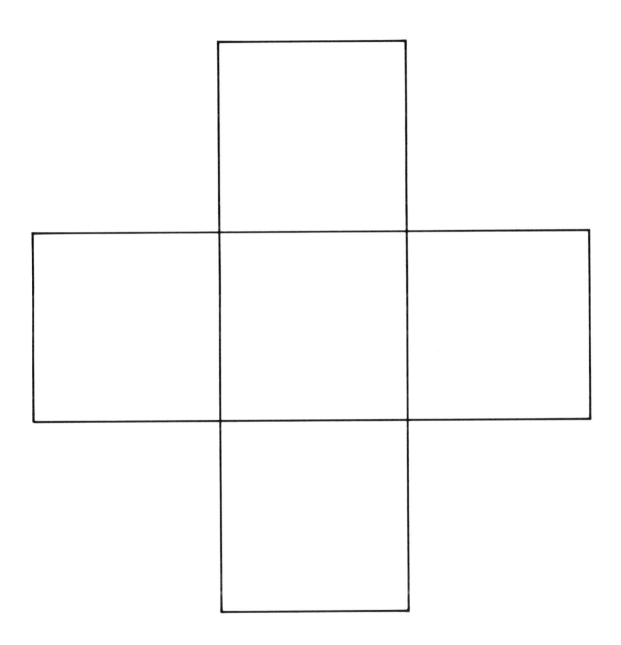

Figure 6

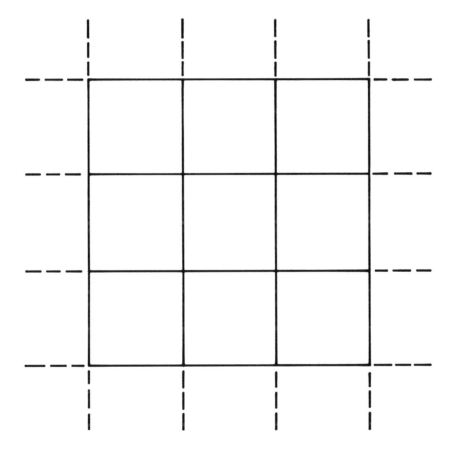

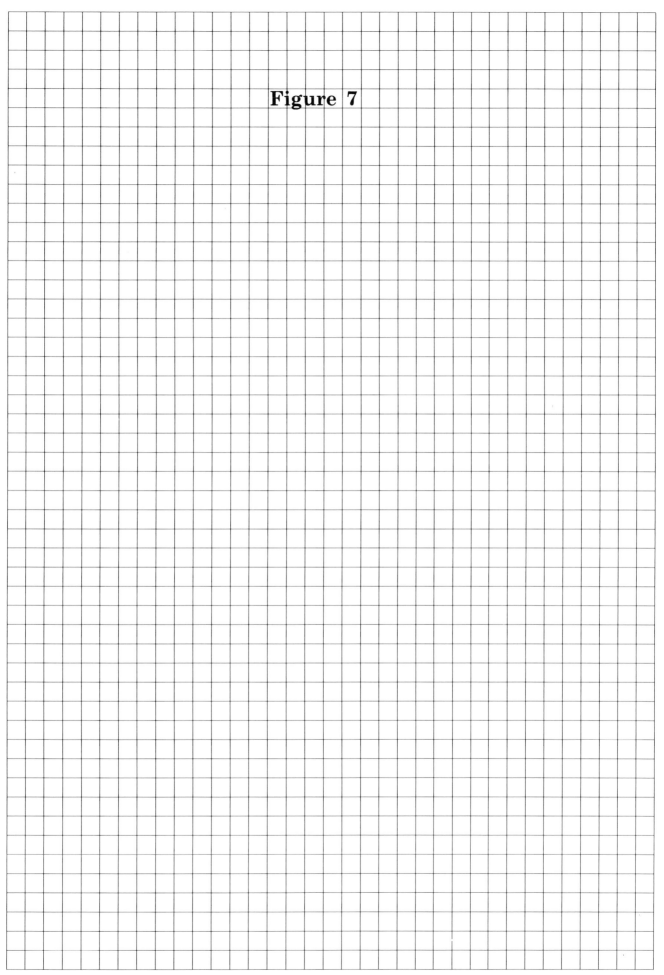
Figure 7

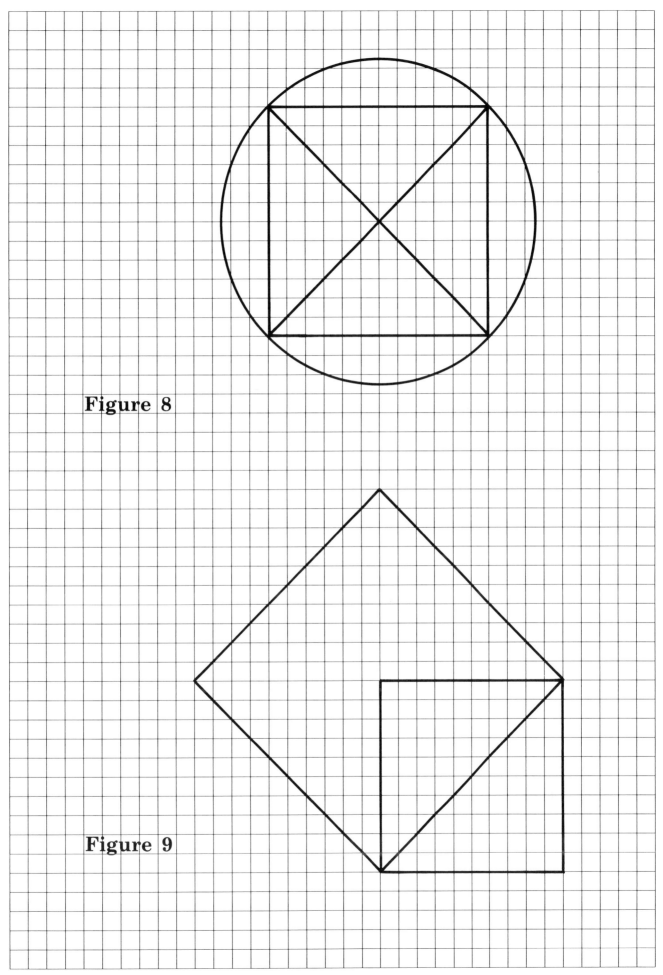

Figure 8

Figure 9

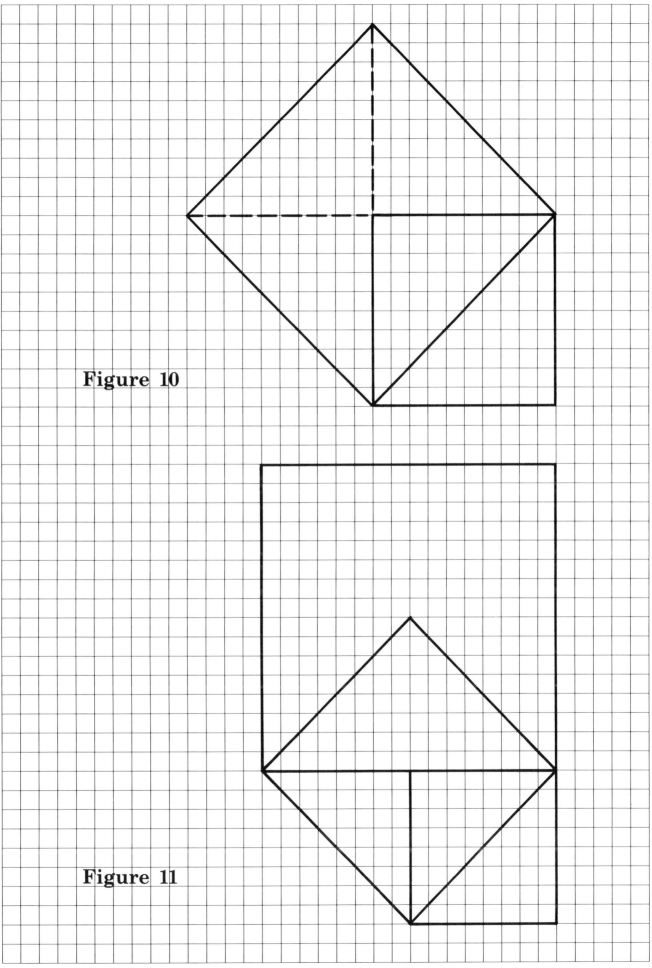

Figure 10

Figure 11

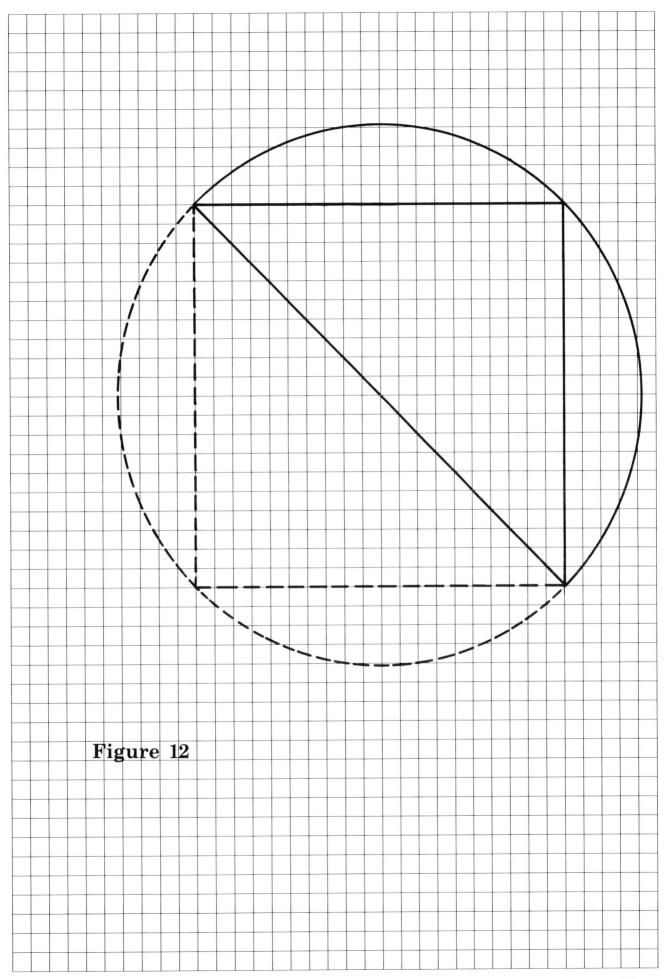

Figure 12

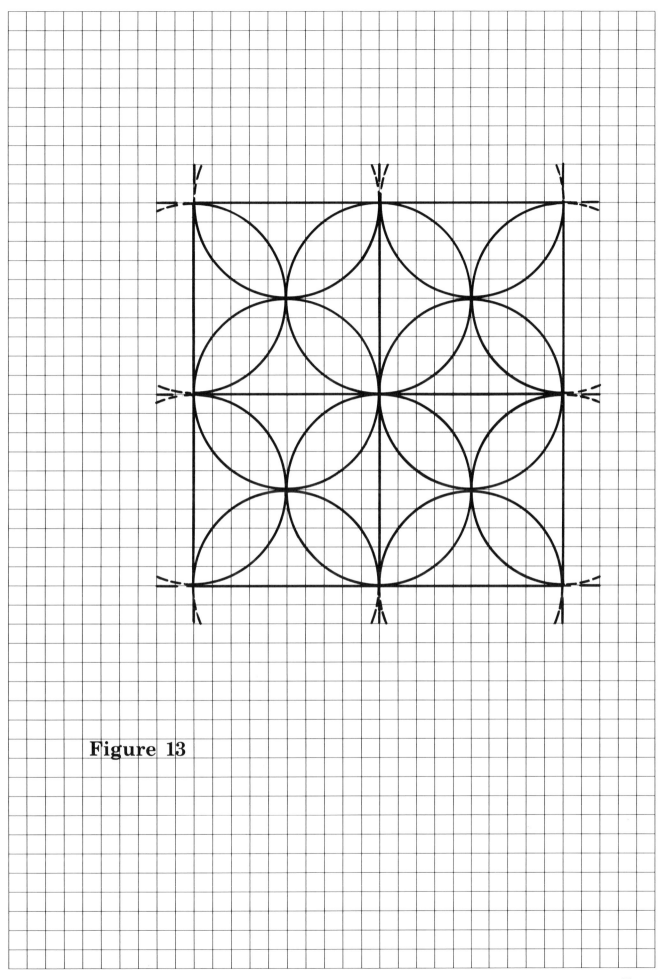

Figure 13

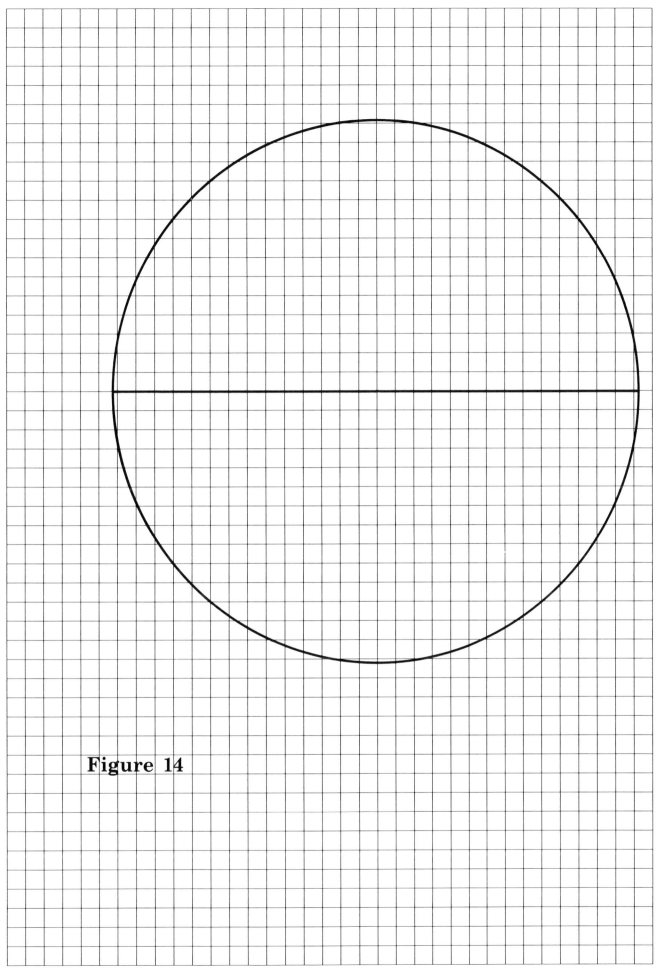

Figure 14

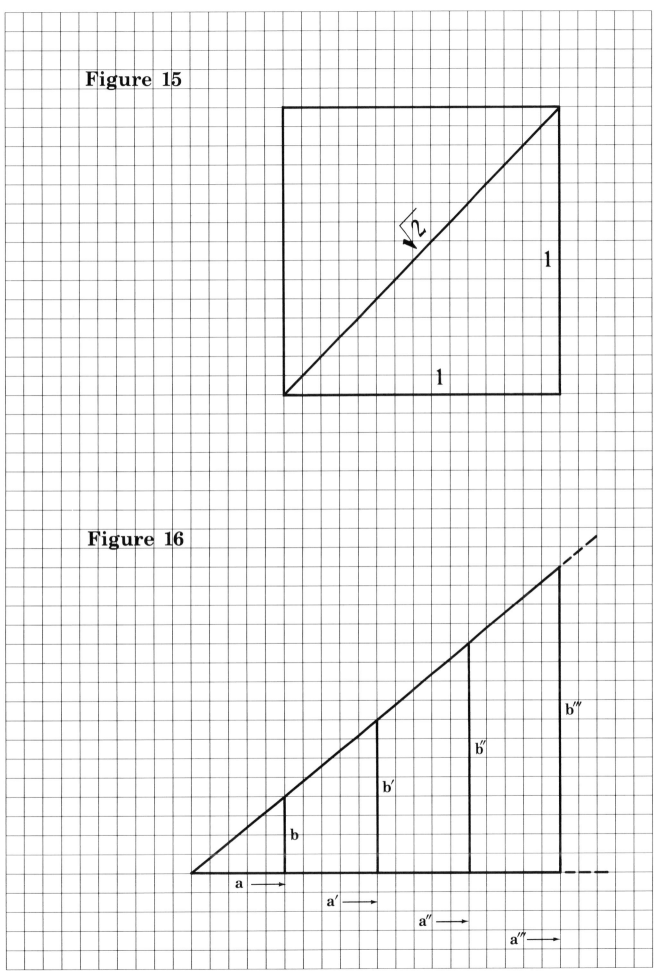

Figure 15

Figure 16

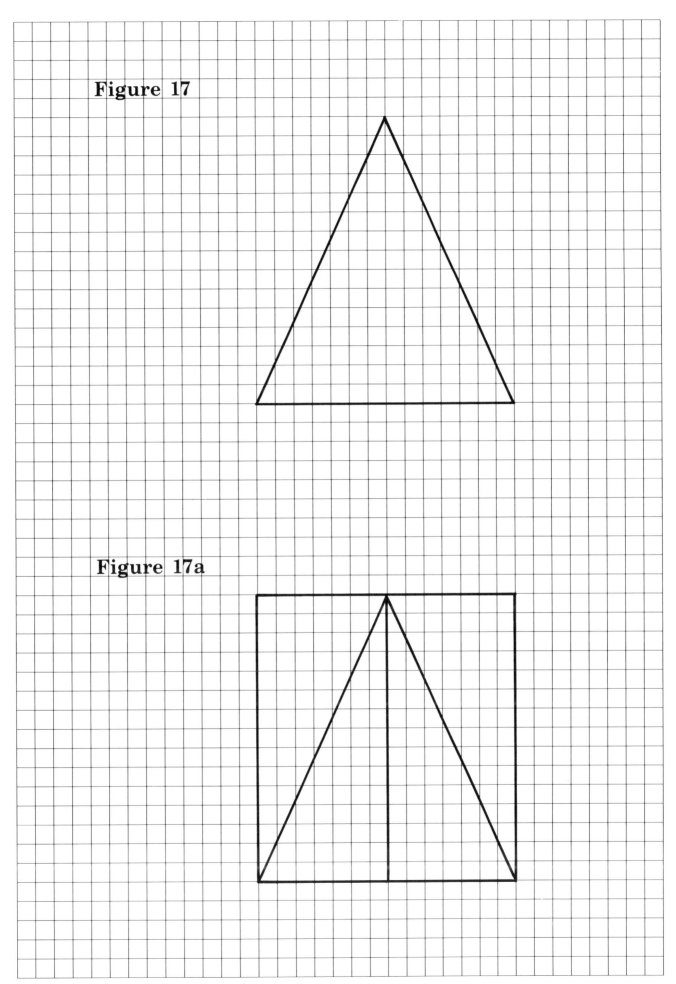

Figure 17

Figure 17a

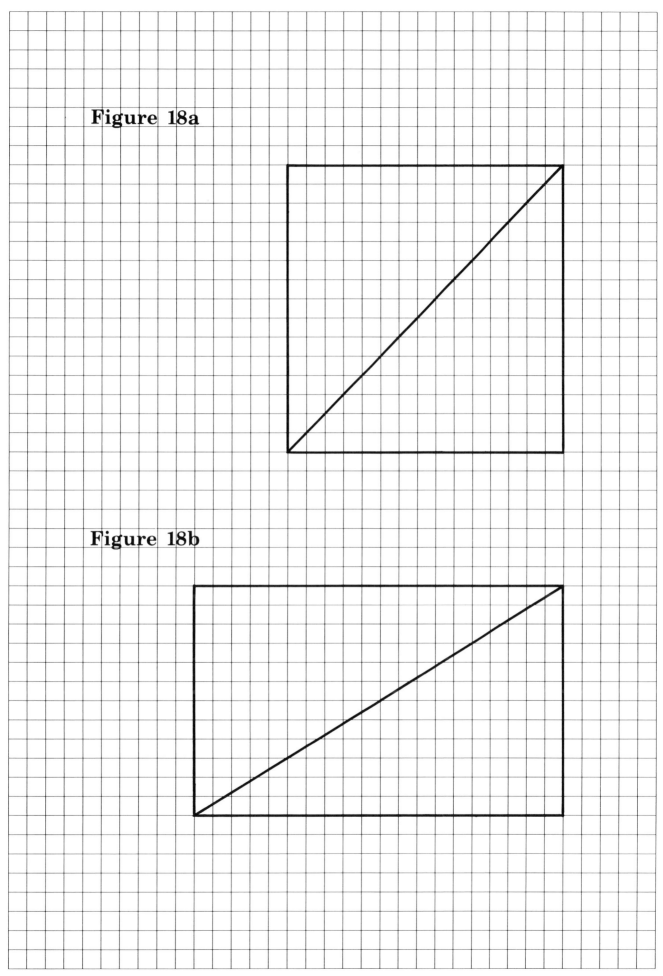

Figure 18a

Figure 18b

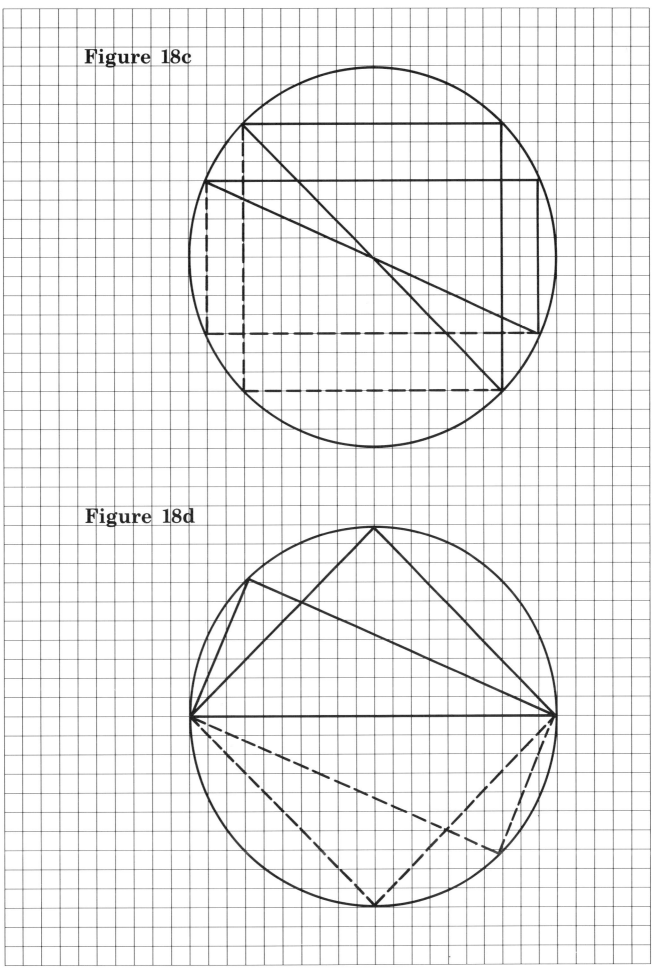

Figure 18c

Figure 18d

109

Figure 18e

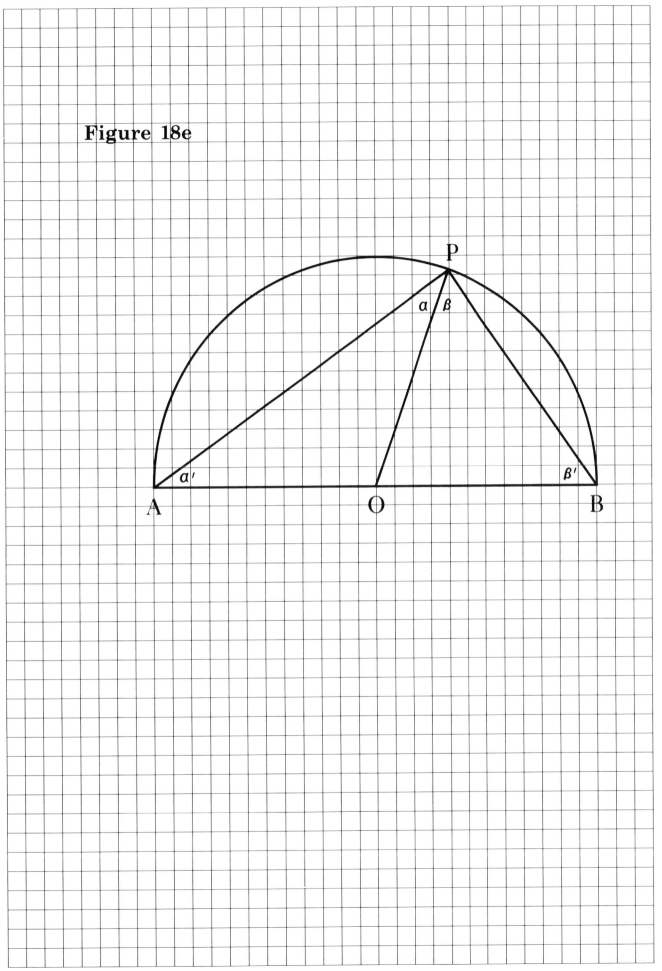

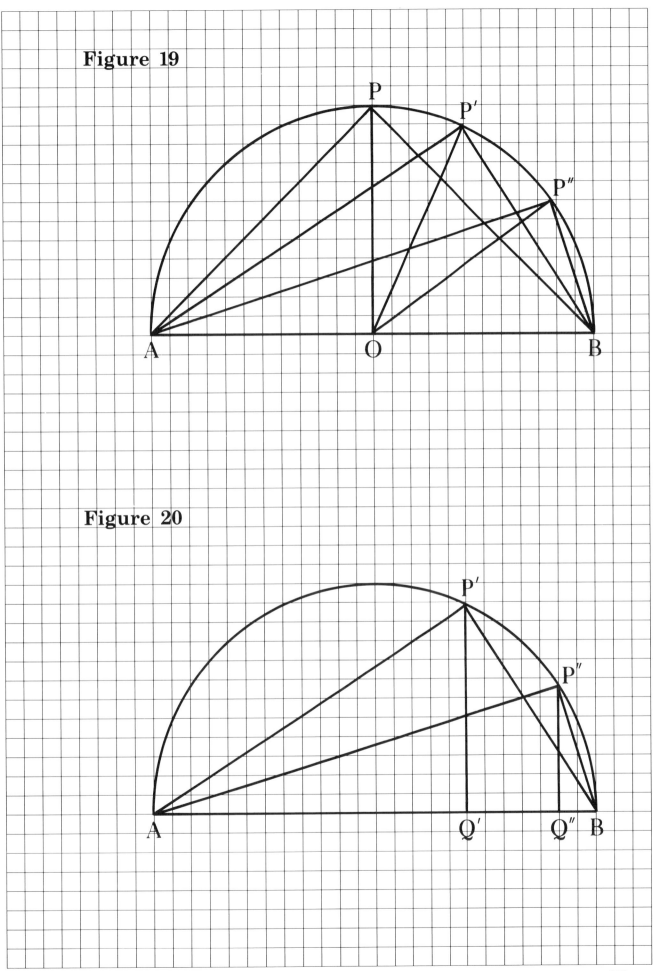

Figure 19

Figure 20

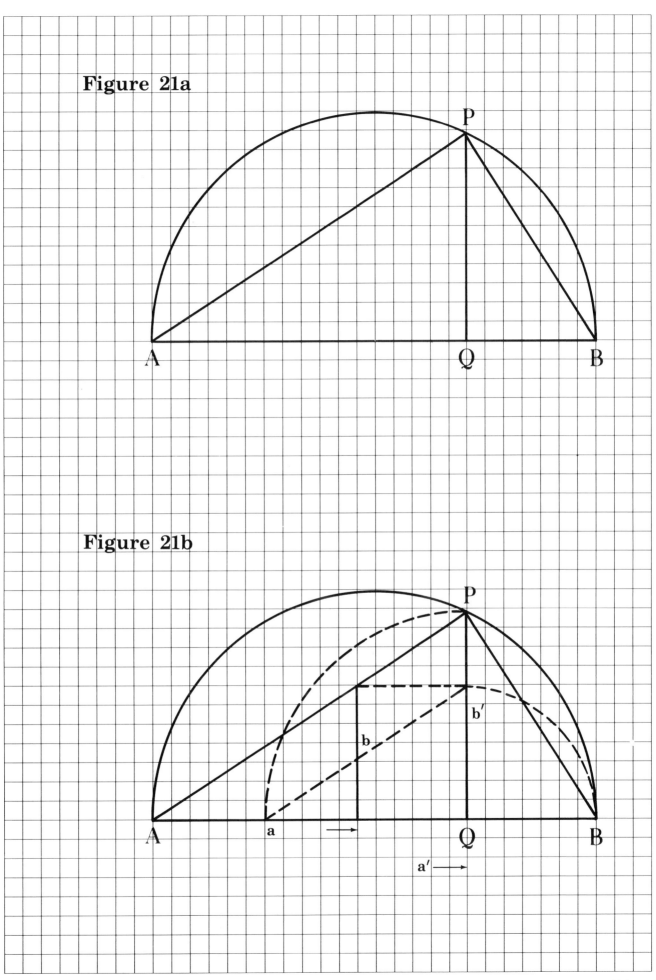

Figure 21a

Figure 21b

Figure 22

Figure 22a

Figure 22b

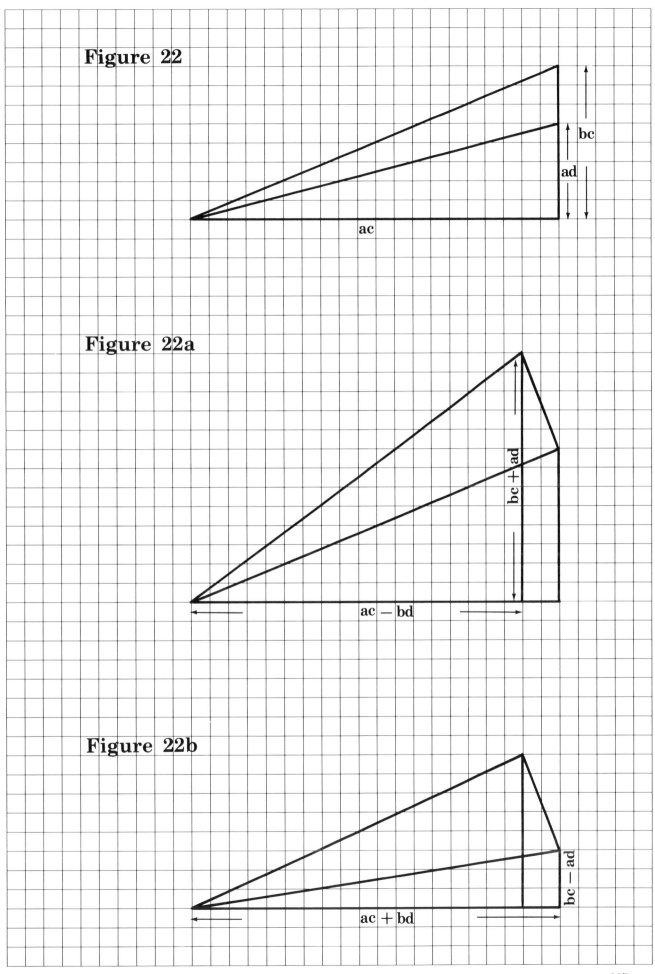

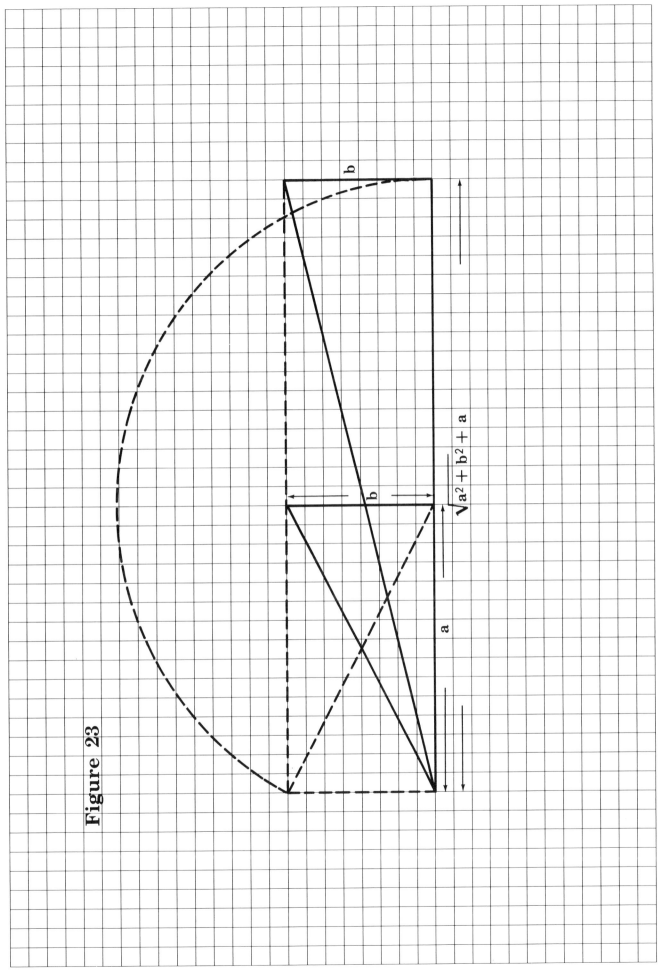

Figure 23

$\sqrt{a^2 + b^2} + a$

a

b

b

119

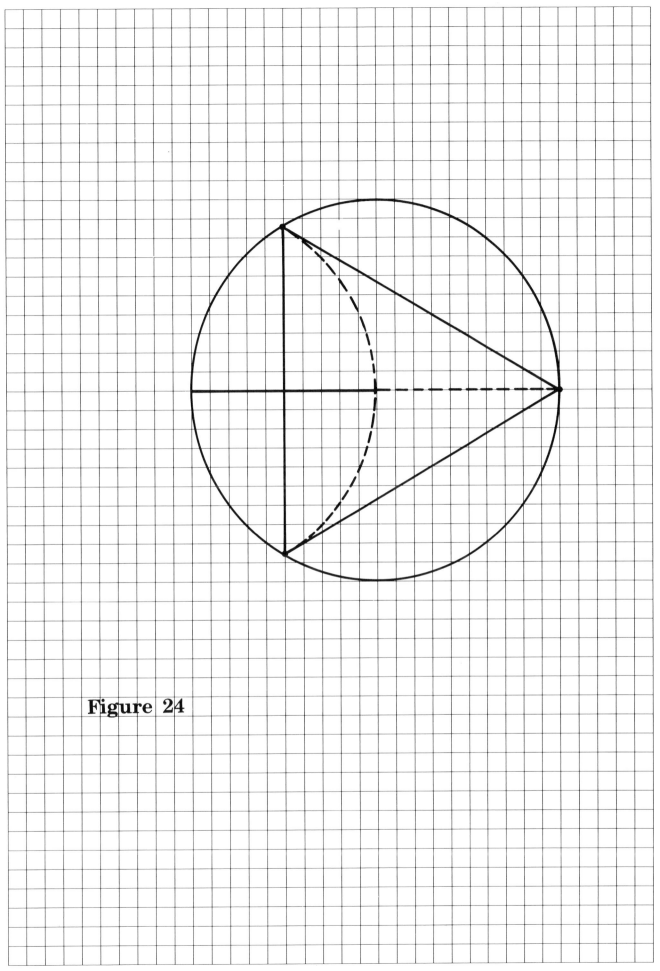

Figure 24

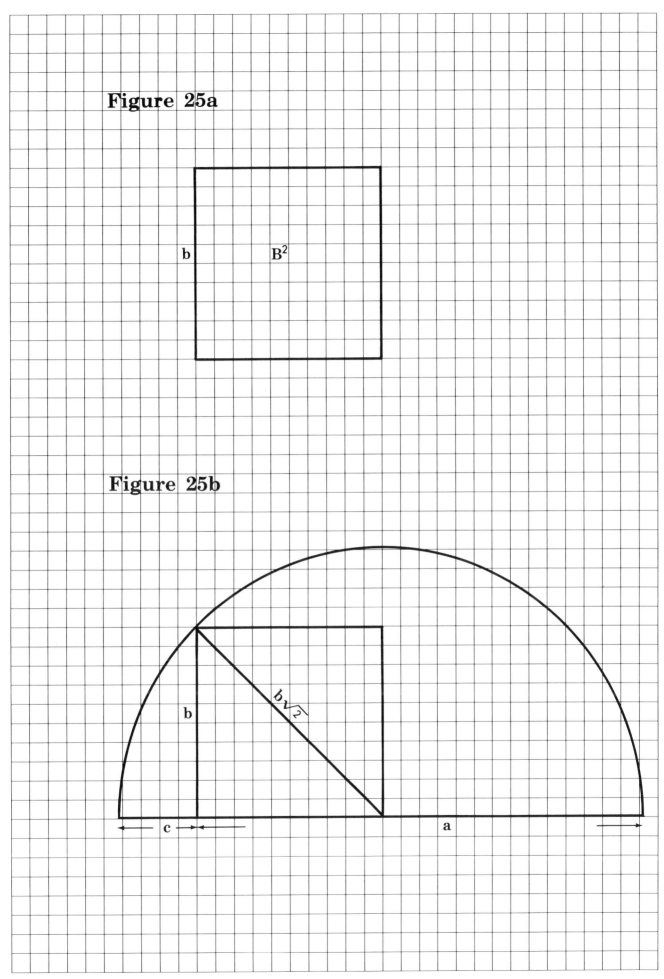

Figure 25a

b B^2

Figure 25b

b $b\sqrt{2}$

c a

123

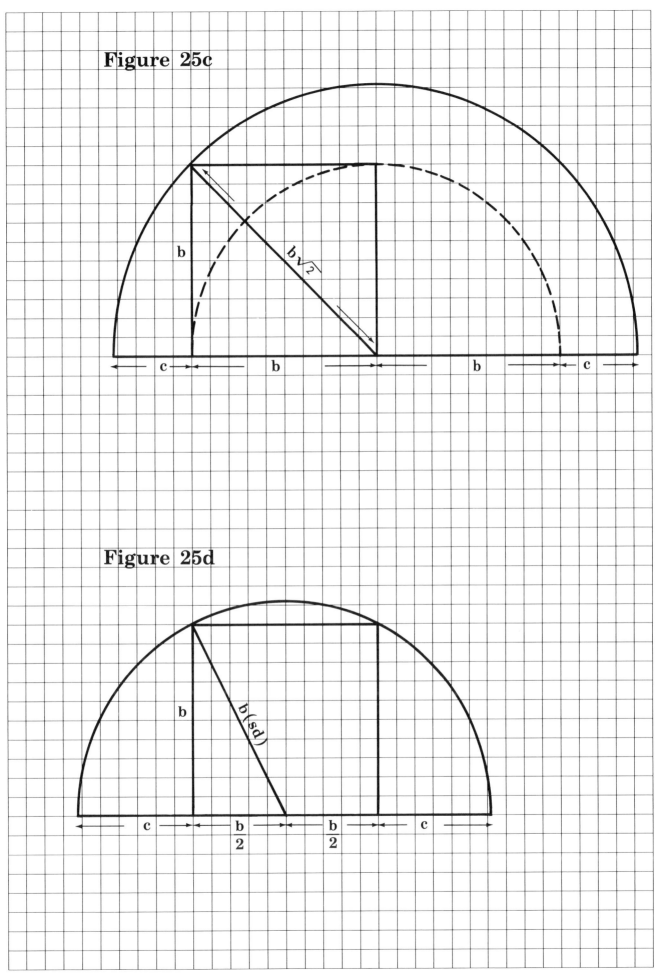

Figure 25c

b

$b\sqrt{2}$

c b b c

Figure 25d

b

$b(sd)$

c $\dfrac{b}{2}$ $\dfrac{b}{2}$ c

Figure 25e

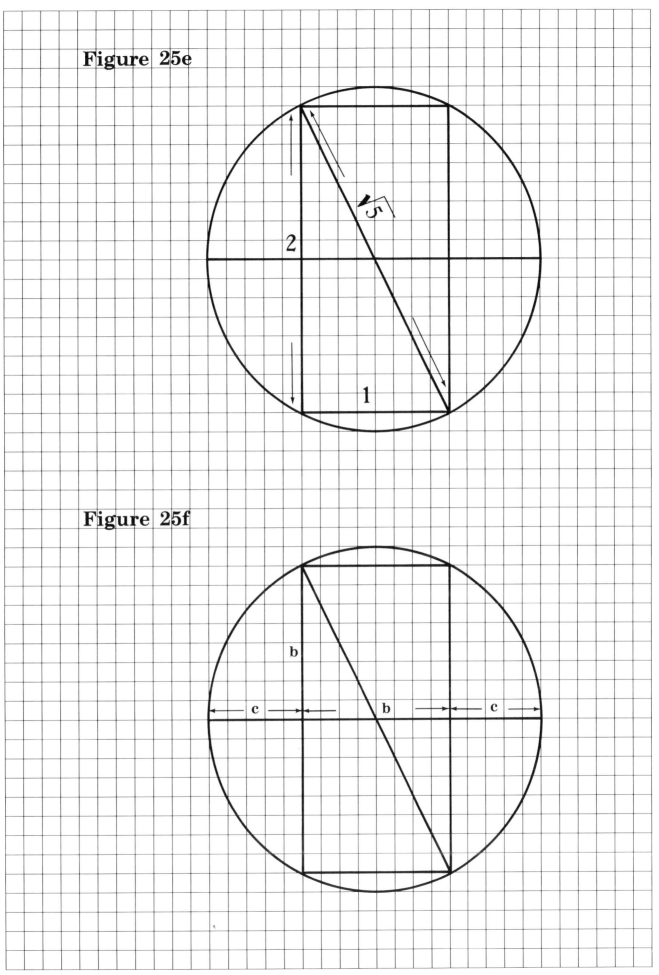

Figure 25f

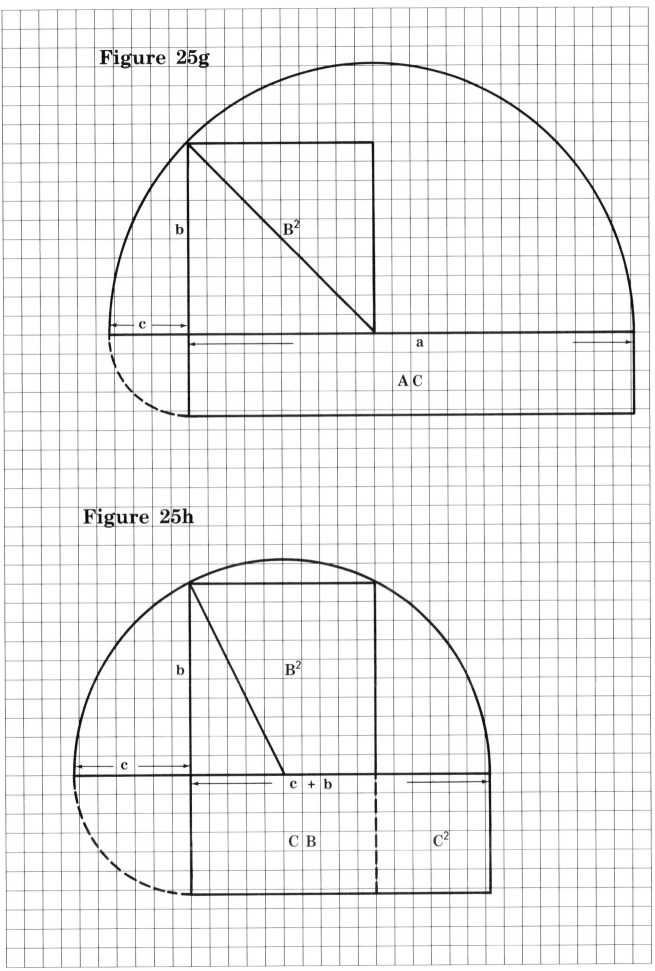

Figure 25g

Figure 25h

129

Figure 25i

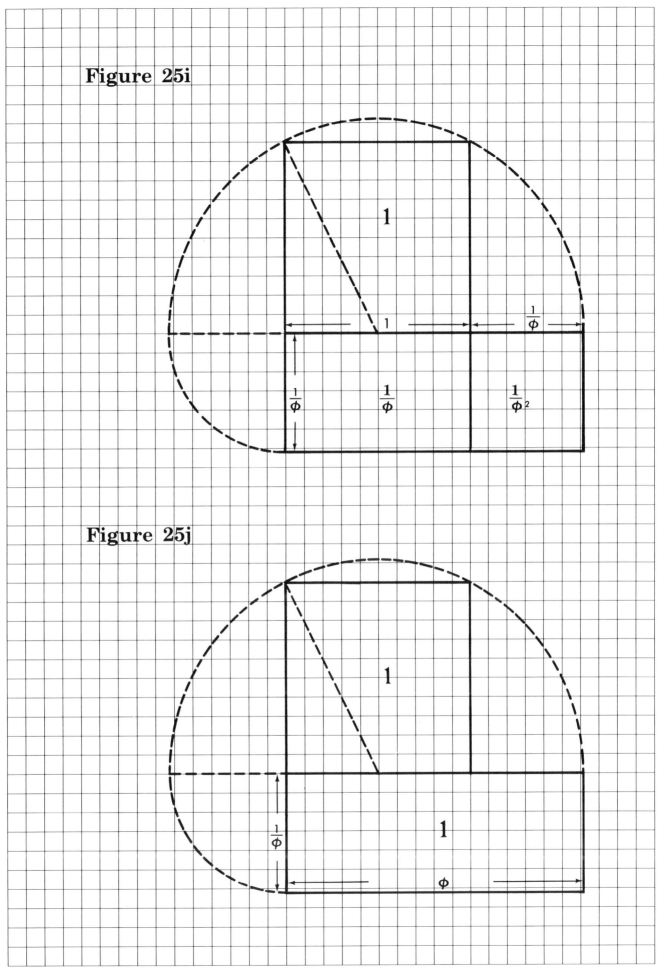

Figure 25j

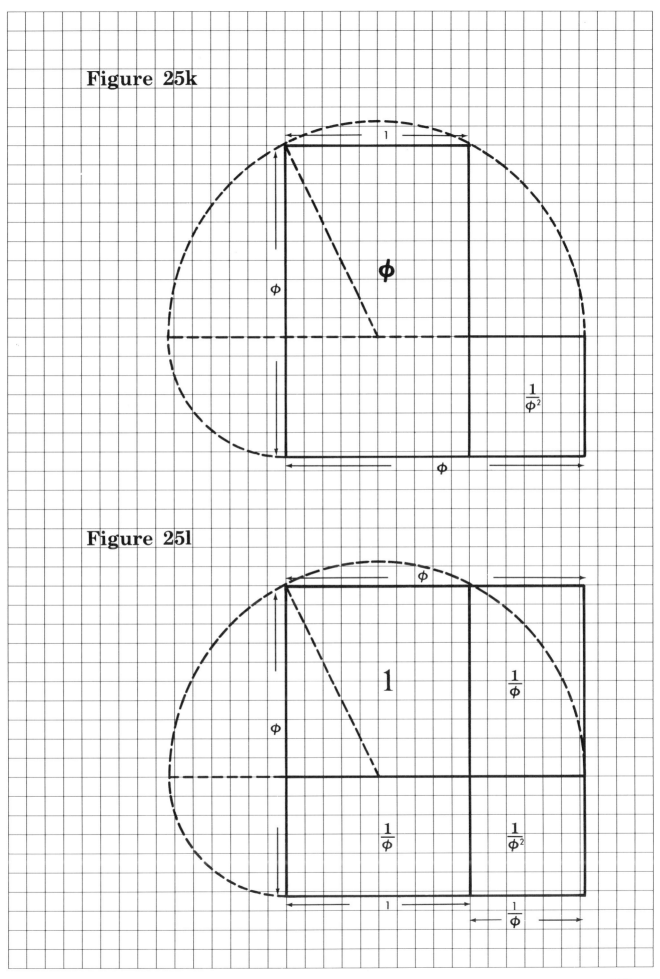

Figure 25k

Figure 25l

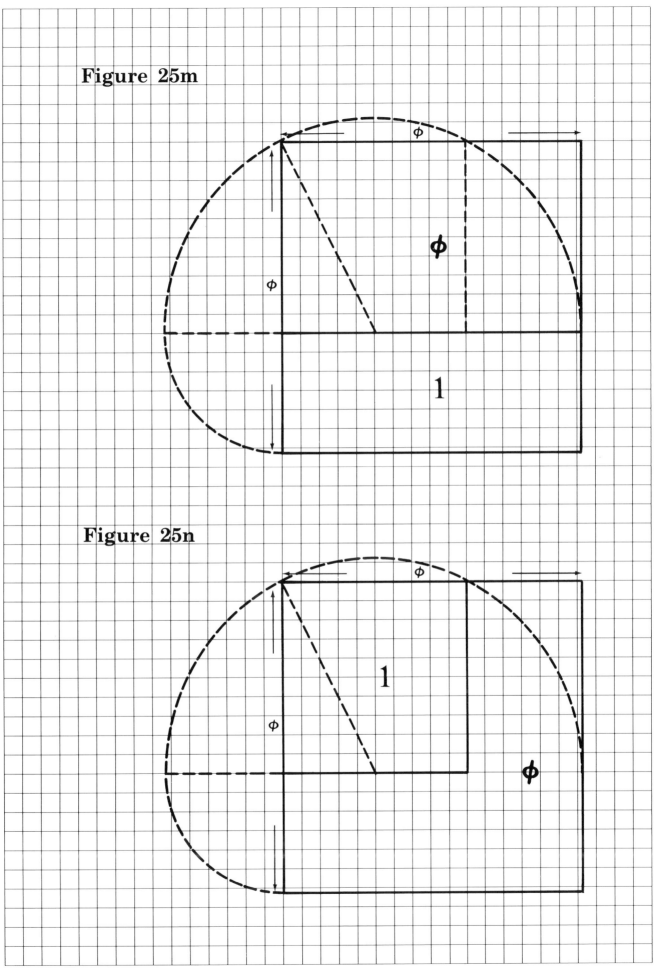

Figure 25m

Figure 25n

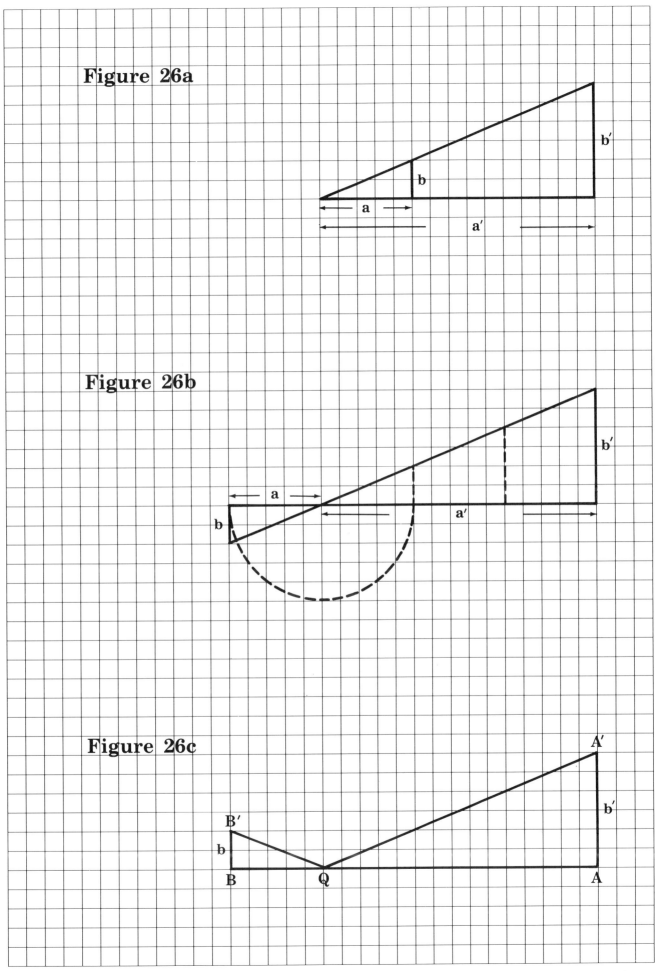

Figure 26a

Figure 26b

Figure 26c

137

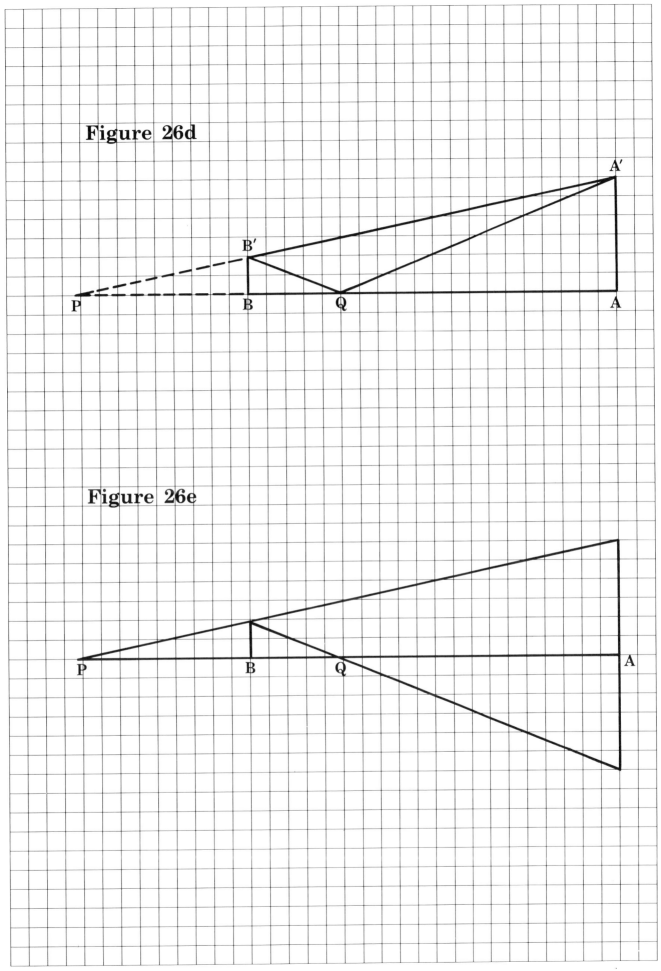

Figure 26d

Figure 26e

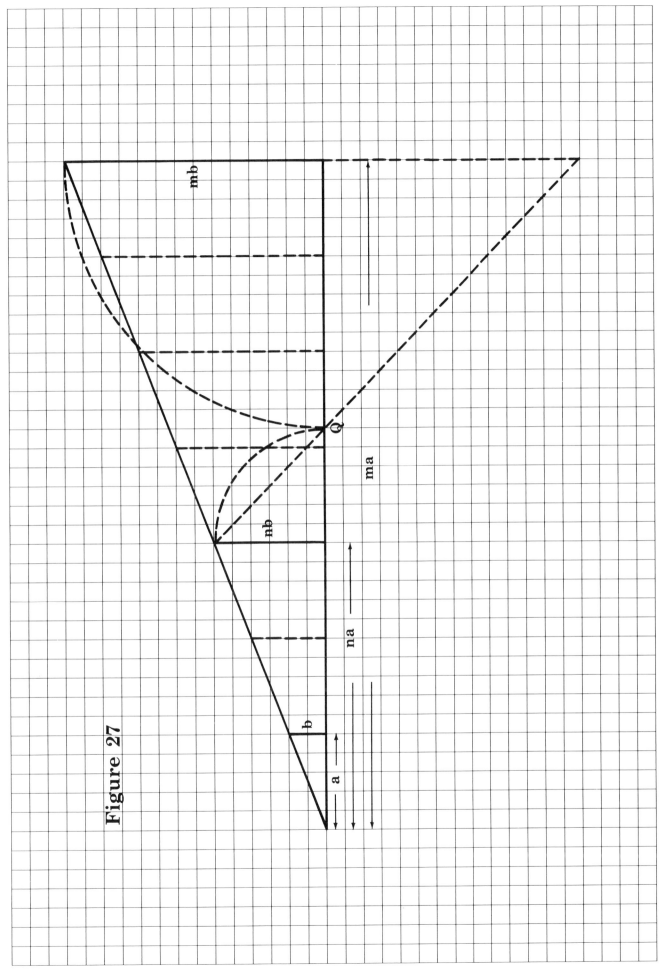

Figure 27

141

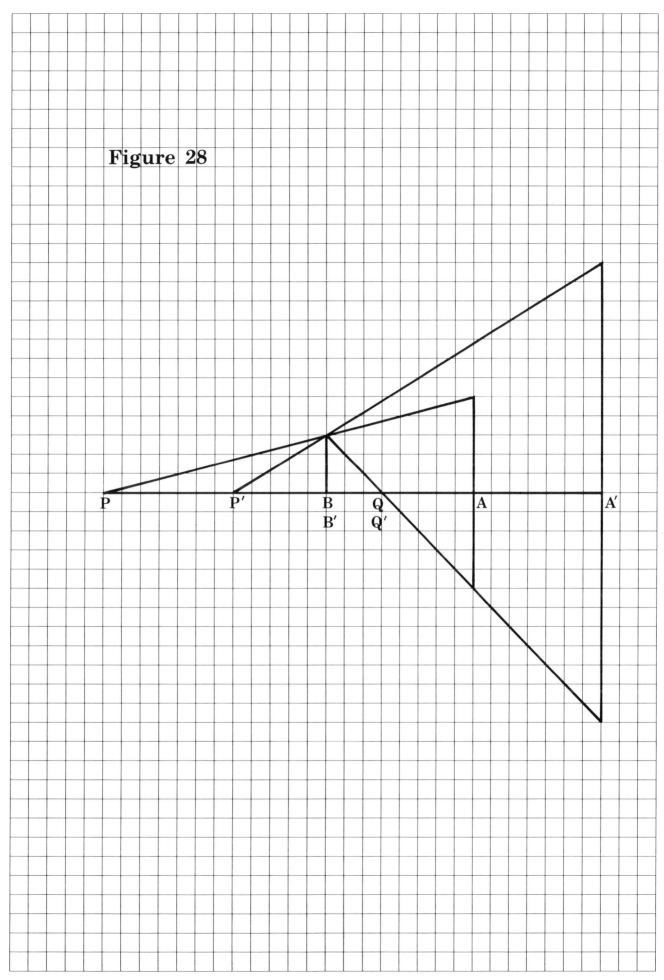

Figure 28

THE BREAD-RATE PROBLEM

THE BREAD-RATE PROBLEM

A COMMENT ON PHARAONIC LOGIC EPITOMIZING THE GEOMETRIC MIND

Problem #72 of the Rhind Mathematical Papyrus reads:

> "Example of exchange of breads for breads. If you are told: 100 breads [of rate] 10 exchanged against a quantity of breads [of rate] 45 . . . ."*

There follows the scribe's operational procedure leading to solution, and a closing text:

> "Then you shall say: it is the exchange of 100 breads [of rate] 10 against 450 breads [of rate] 45, making 10 hekats of wdjyt flour."

The rating of the bread is but the number of breads produced with one hekat† of grain, and a bread rated 10 is *one* bread of the batch of 10 breads produced with *one* hekat of grain, while a bread rated 20, for instance, belongs to a batch of 20 breads produced with the same quantity of grain. Obviously each bread rated 20 is half the size of each bread rated 10, and the higher the rating, the smaller the bread. An inverse relation is established between number and size, an attribute common to all the breads. Typically mathematical in its joining of number to spatial attribute, this relation is antecedent to Problem #72, for we are offered no explanation of the rate notation used in bakeries. And while it is true that such a system must be considered to have been object of common knowledge, it is equally true that this object could become incorporated into a mathematical papyrus only because it was *concretely* rooted and absolutely *non-conventional*. Any rating by convention of a particular product supposes a key to its understanding: asking by brand-name and being told that the product "comes" as #1, #2, #3, and #4, we remain questioning.

Is quality, size, or perhaps shape meant? When *told* that size is meant, we shall still have to be *shown*. Given even the case of a rating hinged onto the metric system, as when 1, 2, 3, and 4 kilos are meant, the rate notation becomes merely

---

* R.A. Schwaller de Lubicz, *Le Temple de L'Homme*, Vol. I., page 247.

† The hekat is the usual Pharonic measure for grain.

less *arbitrary*, yet stays as *conventional* as is the metric system itself. Need of non-conventional rating is not felt in our day, and its possibilities attract no efforts, reflecting the divorce of man from his goods. De Lubicz shows the non-conventional derivation of Pharaonic measure and adaptability of measure to measured product. The *hekat* itself is non-conventional, and the relation between hekat and rating is concrete.*

The theological derivation of the hekat (-measure) is not of concern here. The relation between rating and size, however, is well within our subject and seems to reveal a thought-structure willfully imposed in the face of *impracticability*. Only lastingly deep-seated structures would be sufficiently compelling to overcome the daily incongruence with practical use which the bread-rate system implies. Were we forced to conjecture, we would hold this system to be devised by a *baker* rather than by a *seller* of bread; it was probably "devised" by neither, and possibly strict theological dictate. How, indeed, is the process from grain to bread abstracted in the mind which devises this rating system? Keeping in mind the particular role played by grain in Kemit† as well as in other symboliques, we readily assimilate the measure of grain with a *liquid* measure, as the grain heap receives *form* through the measuring container that gives a unity to grain, which it lacks as heap. Grain, like sand, has some attributes of water. When the grain is in its measure, it encompasses *all* that will come forth from it—a universe measured by the hekat of grain—and the grain is in its measure for one purpose only: to produce a non-definite number of breads, a fact which the Pharaonic rating system never allows us to forget. When we are saying "rate n," we are brought back to a hekat of grain out of which "n" breads came. It seems but one step from here to the formulation of an original hekat *divided* into "n" breads, each bread being 1/nth of the original hekat, the original hekat thus being *one*, and yet, in the propositional sequence, this step does not feel coercive; it certainly does not shoulder its way into the *contemporary* mind. Still, it is plainly the *Pharaonic* thought, with predilection for fractional notation barely concealed. It arrives directly at a fractional expression for each bread because the ingrained structure is the Pharaonic concept of *number*, a divisional-fractional structure, and because no structure marks the mind more sharply than number. The Pharaonic concept of number blends with theology: a universe of fractional entities all having *1* as numerator, a universe created by initial and progressive division of unity so that each entity is a part and part of the whole which is One.

The bread-rate system shows us a particular linking of number with space through the mean term of *rate*, number applied to magnitude not as *measure*, but as *name*. The breads are actually *called* 10-breads, or 45-breads; it is their

---

* Ibid., page 181: *Des volumes pharaoniques.*

† The glyphic name for Pharaonic Egypt.

family-name, in our terms, the common denominator within one hekat. This is the view of a mind which manipulates; it is the baker's approach. To the seller of bread this nomenclature is extraneous. He needs a *price* for his bread and we can follow the path his mind must take to obtain price indication from rate number. If numerical and within barter or a monetary system, a price index must comply with a basic exigence: numerical increase *must* represent increase in value. An inverse notation would necessitate an additional operation before use, namely the operation of inversing the index. And this is indeed the case with the bread index. Buyer or seller, when referring to the index, reaches a conclusion from rate to value only after a reference to the operation which divides a hekat of grain into a certain number of parts represented by breads. If we assume such a rating system to be comprehended as a helpful instrument of daily use, we postulate a mind diametrically opposed to ours, and for all practical purposes we close the book on the possibility of fathoming that mind's motives with any degree of accuracy. But if we see the instrument imposing itself not only in spite of a lack of facility, but positively as an *obstacle* to practical use, then we admit the esoteric grip on the mind of such a structure, a grip from which our present formation permits us to escape: such a system, to our mind, is not reasonable. It contradicts not only *reason*, however, but the persistent and insufficiently documented contention of *empiricism* as touchstone of Pharaonic mentality as well. Thus a working hypothesis leads to incomprehension or misinterpretation unless the notion of empiricism is strictly confined to the limits of *concreteness*, a non-philosophical term, that is to say unless the notion of empiricism is reduced to its very negation. The relation "grain-bread" is a concrete relation, but the mind which construed the rating system *from* that relation is empirical least of all. It may be dogmatic, and it certainly is bent to abstraction, but never, on the strength of this particular product, could it be termed *empirical,* as it flaunts its immunity to contradiction in *experience*. This mind *suffers* experience, but offers it no field of influence.

Rate, then, plays mediety to two extremes, a unitary hekat of grain and a number of breads. The relation of hekat to rate (1:R or 1/R) *names* the bread. The bread has been determined by number, meaning that it has been measured, but the measuring number does not express a *multiplicity of units of measurement,* as when number indicates multiples of grams, kilos, or meters, for instance, but a *multiplicity within an original unity* which gives *measure* without appearing as *measurement*. Once the hekat has measured the grain, has put the grain in its measure, it vanishes as a unit of measurement, as it is inadequate for measuring its own product. Facility in practical use would here dictate a step: the introduction of a measure based on convention, on weight, for instance, so that the weight of each bread in the different number groups would be determined; a weight scale could double as a price scale, because weight and value are in direct relation. This step, bypassed in the bread-rate system, forms for *contemporary* mind a fairly coercive proposition. For Pharaonic thought, measure is contained within the initial unity. A 20-bread is not a size 20 bread, or else a size 40 bread would be twice as large, heavy, or long. A 20-bread is merely a bread named 20, and rate bears a close resemblance to natural number.

The data to Problem #72 is twofold, requiring acquaintance with the bread-rate system as well as with the text set forth by the papyrus; both elements are necessary and sufficient for stating and solving Problem #72. The implicated part of the data consists of a primordial *relation* that the problem uses as prelusive knowledge in the search for *proportion*. We are presented with a logical implication as to the nature of relation while being shown explicitly the path toward proportion. One loses the genetic aspect of mind when leaving such a delicate process unformulated, obscured, and automatized into a puppet manipulating its own strings down the centuries until it has become a sight too familiar to beg comment; yet, a fresher mind might intuit, held by this Polichinello, a vital clue to the workings of man's reason. And can we not, already now, expect to find *that* intuition responsible for Problem #72? A problem? An example* of exchange of bread for bread, but an example which never finds occasion for observance in the remaining text of the papyrus.† No other problem is solved along these lines. As example, Problem #72 is unnecessary, and as a problem it does not exist. What problem? Its terms cannot be tackled without the key to the bread-rate system, and yet it stops being a problem as soon as the latter is known, being then solvable at sight. Perfectly transparent for anyone who holds the key, it is desperately opaque for one who doesn't. Problem #72 is the traditional image of the esoteric text, where a reading is either totally absent or brilliantly obvious. Now the reason for its obviousness is curious: it lies in the *impracticability* of the example. Indeed, if we exchange breads for breads, the index, *being a number of breads*, works in a direct relation to the number of breads exchanged. Ten breads rated 10 are obviously equivalent to 45 breads rated 45, being the production of one hekat of grain. The index seems definitely geared toward exchanges of *bread* for *bread*, and yet, barring exchanges of bakery stocks, it is difficult to conjure up occasions for this application: Problem #72 must be admitted as being theoretical through and through. by and large, bread must have been exchanged against other commodities and we have no evidence of bread as currency in ancient Egypt. It then becomes of interest to examine *ritual* for such occurrences, to question glyphs in scenes of *offerings* when breads are concerned, searching for a possible reading of *exchange*, a valid hypothesis, as movement is rarely one-sided in glyphic offering.

* the glyph *tp* (a face in profile) here signifies "example of solution." Ibid., page 247 ff.

† "Problem #72, the first in this series, is given as example (tp) and yet it is treated completely differently, as it plays on the differences . . ." *Ibid.*, page 246.

At this time we would do well to remind ourselves that the discussion of Problem #72 is based upon the notion of *rate*, a concept belonging to the limitations of the version rather than to the original glyphs. Let us bring forward the picture groups responsible for this injected concept:

(a)   100 breads [of rate] 10

(b)   a quantity of breads [of rate] 45

and after the solution of the problem, the closing text:

(c)   Then you shall say: it is the exchange of 100 breads [of rate] 10 against 450 breads [of rate] 45, making 10 hekats of wdjyt flour.

These groups of signs read literally:

(a)   breads 10 R 100

(b)   a quantity of breads 45

(c)   ... the exchange of breads 10 R 100 against breads 45 R 450.

The sole basis for the translation "rate" is the sign transliterated as "R," the glyph with phonetic value of "R," and a sign included in the hieroglyphic alphabet.

Among the many meanings which converge on this glyph,* its use as a fractional sign is here of particular interest. Placed below the sign, a numeral will indicate the number of equal parts into which unity is divided, in practice thus taking a value comparable to an expression 1/n in our system. In practice only, though, for we must retain the theoretical dissimilarity of a notation precluding the use of numerators other than unity, and precluding it so severely and consistently as to render superfluous the very indication of the unitary numerator itself. Were it not for the theologically induced inability of the Pharaonic mind to conceive multiplicity in any way save through the division of one-ness, "rate" could be interpreted as numerator and the number of breads as denominator. Statement of the problem would then essentially reduce to:

$$\frac{10}{100} \text{ exchanged against } \frac{45}{x}.$$

---

* mouth, word, speech, entrance, opening, gate, et. al.

Such an arrangement of the given terms seems to leap to the eye; yet its expression is unknown to glyphic philology.

At this time and before broaching the Pharaonic calculator's solution to Problem #72, it would be well to epitomize the aims of this study and the questions which it attempts to clarify. We seek an appreciation of the bread-rate system as a tool for anchoring theological conduct of mind to daily necessity. The intent of Problem #72 may well be to impose upon the reader, in the face of far simpler and even obvious solutions, a course of action, complex indeed, but theologically motivated. This would ease a comprehension on two topics: the choice of an exchange of breads against breads as an example of what we construe as a problem of proportion, and the relatively complex mode of solution in a problem solvable at sight. Discussion of Problem #72 hopes to clarify the import to Pharaonic thought of relation and proportion in general.

According to de Lubicz, the steps to solution taken by the calculator show implicit knowledge of one of the properties of proportions, namely:

> In any proportion, the sum or difference of the two first terms is to the second as the sum or difference of the two last terms is to the fourth.*

While a rote solution based on this formula would indeed follow the lines established in the papyrus, several factors plead for a deeper understanding of the calculator's intention.

The sequence of operations leading to solution is as follows:

(a) $45 - 10 = 35$

(b) $35 : 10 = 3\frac{1}{2}$

(c) $100 \times 3\frac{1}{2} = 350$

(d) $350 + 100 = 450.$

A concluding text sums up:

> Then you shall say: it is the exchange of the 100 breads [of rate] 10 against 450 breads [of rate] 45, being 10 hekats of wdjyt flour.

---

* Ibid., page 246.

It has been argued that no hieroglyphic text so far deciphered can possibly be interpreted as a compilation of theoretical data or of abstract laws to cover a variety of applications, and that only particular representations of immediate experience seem to fall within the realm or potentiality of Pharaonic speculations. While the Pharaonic method seems indeed unwilling to separate qualities or relations from representations and thus never compiles abstract material, teachings on a high level of abstraction invariably overshadow the particular glyphic representation. Futile discussions ensue from conjectures as to whether or not the properties of proportions were known to the author of the papyrus; there is no doubt that Problem #72 duplicates the steps of a solution based on one of these properties. As it corresponds exactly to the steps dictated by the law, the conclusion is easily drawn that it *instances* this law, although such a conclusion foists upon our subject a conduct incompatible with his mentality. The absence of theoretical works in Kemit is a fact to be used as auxiliary argument only. Of primary importance is the evidence that a solution according to the law can be worked out only through the finery of an algebraic set-up and specifically by means of an unknown, an equation, and a shift of a term from one member of the equation to the other, with a consequent change of sign. De Lubicz proposes a geometric solution which skirts these inconveniences, but, while it may well trace a picture of the geometric mentality, it is far too removed from the steps to solution actually indicated by the scribe. When de Lubicz retraces these steps, he is himself unable to avoid the algebraic elements mentioned above.* The expression of the law does indeed impose a picture such as:

$$\frac{45 - 10}{10} \; : \; \frac{x - 100}{100}.$$

The scribe's first two steps reduce this expression to:

$$3\tfrac{1}{2} = \frac{x - 100}{100}.$$

The third step implies cross-multiplication:

$$350 = x - 100.$$

And finally the term "−100" must be shifted to the left side of the equation, changing its sign in the process. The entire procedure is unacceptable in light of what is known of Pharaonic notation and mentality.

---

* Ibid., page 247.

Curiously, the impasse encountered shows a foible of *our* intellect as it conde-scends to a prejudged level. Even a superficial study of ancient Egypt proves that with Pharaonic Myth, Architecture, and Art, reason in fact enters an un-known where any judgment can at best be opinion. Now if the aim is knowl-edge, it may either reside in knowing what part of the foreign mind coincides with ours, or else it may be guided toward knowing the part that is beyond us. The first is a study of the known and a contribution to History, the second of the unknown and a contribution to consciousness. Neither approach should be neglected for the sake of the other. A sound reading of Problem #72 must be strictly reined to the confines of the mentality which authored the text. Needless to say, a probe into so foreign a mind suffers no preconceptions, no foregone conclusions; and yet, despite ourselves, our cultural habits and idiosyncracies tend to intrude into our appreciations. Studies of Problem #72 thus have im-plicitly (or at least unconsciously) divided the problem into three parts: (1) an introductory proposition, (2) the main body of the text, and (3) a concluding statement. For all logical purposes only (2) has received attention. A stylistic preconception rooted in our own expository conventions, this tripartite reading neglects the logical content of (1) and (3) to the extent of clouding the meaning of the text as a whole. (1) initiates the text, announcing an example of exchange of breads for breads. Nowhere is it implied that the problem exemplifies a general method beyond bread-exchanges; nowhere is there evidence that the Pharaonic calculator's concern is with proportionality; and nothing leads us to assume, either in the text or from what is known of the mentality we are study-ing, that other commodities are to be exchanged in the manner exemplified by bread-exchange. To the contrary, the uniqueness of the bread-rate system weighs in favor of a unique method restricted to the exchange of breads for breads. To envision (2) as anything else but an example of bread-exchange hence leads to logical error. The problem does not show a particular property of proportions; it shows an exchange of breads. Within the context of the papyrus as a whole, it must be considered meaningful that no other problem involving proportional exchanges is solved along the lines of Problem #72. To assume a deep-rooted, hence probably theological reason for the particular line of solution is thus heuristically valid. The salient difference between Greek and Pharaonic mind springs to the fore: the former would consider the problem as instancing a general property of proportions, the latter sees a particular conduct of rigidly limited scope. The mathematical character of generality is useless to the Egyp-tian, as the specific procedure means only to solve the particular problem of exchanging breads. The inductive process is stymied by the necessity of re-stricting a particular approach to its consecrated use.

The challenge of the reading, therefore, is to fathom the bread-exchange by means of the lines of the solution. Knowledge of the four arithmetical opera-tions, and acquaintance with the bread-rate system are necessary and sufficient to measure our sounding. Thus equipped, we read once more the lines of the solution:

$$\text{(a)} \quad 45 - 10 = 35.$$

The calculator compares the two rates and finds that 35 more breads are produced by each "hekat of the unknown quantity" than by each "hekat of the known quantity":

$$\text{(b)} \quad 35 : 10 = 3\tfrac{1}{2}.$$

In order to appreciate this step in its pragmatic simplicity, it is helpful to visualize the hekats. Here are the products of one "hekat of the known quantity," a row of 10 large-sized breads, and over there, the products of one "hekat of unknown quantity," a row of 45 small-sized breads. Operation (b) now distributes the excedent of "the hekat of the unknown quantity" into "the hekat of the known quantity," piling up $3\tfrac{1}{2}$ small breads next to every one of the 10 large breads. Now this amounts to just one thing: the "hekat of the unknown quantity" has been given the internal structure of the "hekat of the known quantity." The hekats have been made to look alike. This gives the basic unit of a "hekat of the unknown quantity" in the form of a "hekat of the known quantity," namely $(1 + 3\tfrac{1}{2})$ that needs only to be taken 100 times to obtain the result. The scribe first multiples the excedent by 100:

$$\text{(c)} \quad 100 \times 3\tfrac{1}{2} = 350$$

Then adds 100

$$\text{(d)} \quad 350 + 100 = 450$$

and in his concluding sentence, specifies that 10 hekats of flour were involved in the exchange. This statement and its polarity with the introductory proposition give the key to the metaphysical lesson. The specified objects through which the matter of the problem was presented vanish into the nonspecified materia whence they arose. Mention of the hekat abruptly illumines the horizon of identity that precedes all rating and within which the problem of exchange dissolves. There remains an exchange of 10 hekats of wdjyt flour, a transaction presenting no problem, and barely deserving the name of exchange. As we now review the steps of the solution, we see more clearly the calculator's operations *within* the hekat, his structural rearranging of an *apparent* multiplicity within the enveloping unity of the basic measure. The true nature of the bread-rate is underlined, not a number, but a particular structure of *relative unity*, the potential multiplicity of a unity susceptible to scission. As long as this unity is recalled, multiplicity is held in check.

Thus the bread-rate system in simple lines and in a medium of daily popular concern, sketches the framework of the most fundamental mythical intuition. Problem #72 may well serve as a reminder to keep this intuition alive. For upon its life depends the life of Pharaonic theocracy.